MANAGING TO PEAK PERFORMANCE

Randy D. Shillingburg

Managing to Peak Performance Copyright © 2019
by Randy D. Shillingburg, Shillingburg Consulting.
All Rights Reserved.

All rights reserved. No part of this book may be reproduced in any form or by any electronic or mechanical means including information storage and retrieval systems, without permission in writing from the author. The only exception is by a reviewer, who may quote short excerpts in a review.

Cover designed by Wendy Vandersluis, Vendis Designs
Thank you, Wendy!

Visit our website at:
www.shillingburgconsulting.com

Printed in the United States of America

Second Edition: April 2019
Shillingburg Consulting

For media inquiries, book signings, speaking engagements or management consulting opportunities, contact:

Shillingburg Consulting
10 Mount Vista Drive
Buckhannon, WV 26201
randy@shillingburgconsulting.com
304-389-4038

This book and its contents are dedicated to the people who have been my strongest supporters:

My wife,
Monica Shillingburg

My two sons,
Morgan Shillingburg and Todd Shillingburg

My three sisters,
Melodye Harris, Anita Shillingburg and Faye Shillingburg

My parents,
Betty and Clarence "Mutt" Shillingburg

CONTENTS

Prologue: Managing to Peak Performance 1
Chapter 1: Showing vs. Telling 5
Chapter 2: Leading at an Early Age 13
Chapter 3: Caring about Your Employees 20
Chapter 4: Micromanaging 27
Chapter 5: Maximizing Sales Growth 31
Chapter 6: Winning 38
Chapter 7: Testing Management Philosophies 41
Chapter 8: Developing Employees 45
Chapter 9: Keep It Simple, Stupid 55
Chapter 10: Putting Employees First 63
Chapter 11: People and Numbers 72
Chapter 12: Clear Vision 84
Chapter 13: Learning from Others 89
Chapter 14: Goal Setting 92
Chapter 15: More Winning 96
Chapter 16: Inclusion 99
Chapter 17: Onboarding 110
Chapter 18: Process 114
Chapter 19: Celebrating Victories, Large and Small 120
Chapter 20: Feedback 124
Chapter 21: Organizational Health 131
Chapter 22: Responsibility vs. Authority 134
Chapter 23: No Limits 137
Chapter 24: Inspired Leadership 148
Chapter 25: Looking in the Mirror 156
Chapter 26: Learning from Mistakes 159
Chapter 27: Pulling It All Together 167
Chapter 28: Present because They Were Present 171
Epilogue: They Won't Have a Chance 181

Prologue: Managing to Peak Performance

My professional career is drawing to a close, so I would like to share a little of the knowledge I've gathered along the way to help you become a more effective manager.

During my 37-year professional career, I have had the privilege and honor of leading teams in nearly every type of organization, from Fortune 500 companies to school systems, small businesses, a state department of education and even non-profit organizations.

I have worked directly with or provided consulting services for electric utilities, coal companies, chemical companies, natural gas companies, small businesses, social change organizations, a public relations firm, and even many of the nation's largest school systems, including Los Angeles Unified School District and Miami-Dade County Public Schools. I have even led large groups of employees and managers in a fast-paced, results-based production environment.

Yes, I've pretty much done it all as an executive, manager or consultant. Most importantly, I have learned something important at every stop – and those opportunities have spanned nearly the entire country.

I've worked in Arkansas, California, Connecticut, Delaware, Illinois, Kentucky, Michigan, Minnesota, Montana, New Jersey, New York, North Carolina, Ohio, Pennsylvania, South Carolina, Texas, Virginia, West Virginia, Wisconsin and even Washington, D.C.

Randy D. Shillingburg

I have toiled in some of the most rural communities of America and also in many of our nation's largest metropolitan areas.

Unlike many who manage – who spend their entire careers working with only one or two organizations and learning how to manage in a specific sector or industry – I have been very fortunate to lead people in nearly every type of organization, which has provided me with a unique perspective on management.

At the beginning of my professional career, I thought I would only have the opportunity to work in the electric utility industry. I thoroughly enjoyed this challenging work and was a natural at communicating during crises such as ice storms, snow storms and hurricanes. But a corporate downsizing as a result of an office merger pushed me out of my comfort zone into varied and even more challenging positions that allowed me to learn and grow as a leader.

Looking back now, I realize how severely limited my management experience would have been if I had only been exposed to that one industry. I am positive that if I had not been downsized, I would have worked for the same utility for 30 years – and would have only learned how to manage in that industry. Since being downsized, though, I have enjoyed a myriad of opportunities that have allowed me to see a wide spectrum of management styles and philosophies.

I can now see that being downsized was truly a blessing in disguise. At every opportunity – whether working directly with or providing consulting services for dozens of organizations – I have been able to learn something important about management.

I have also had the chance to learn from hundreds of wonderful co-workers, mentors and clients, many of whom are recognized on these pages. Looking back on my career while writing this book, I began to realize just how blessed I have been to work with so many driven, insightful and intelligent people. In many ways, "Managing to Peak Performance" is a "Thank You!" and sincere tribute to those people who have guided, supported and inspired me.

Time and time again, I have seen that quality, effective management makes a dramatic difference in the performance of *any* organization. I have also seen that there are many more striking similarities than dramatic differences in effective management across all market sectors.

MANAGING TO PEAK PERFORMANCE

At nearly every stage of my career, I have been able to guide organizations to unparalleled success in terms of teamwork, sales and revenues. Especially in the latter half of my career, I developed a skill for bringing people together, facilitating decision-making and helping teams accomplish more than probably even employees themselves believed they could achieve. In the last several years, I accepted positions I likely would have never even applied for when I was younger, but I wanted *different challenges* and the opportunity to *broaden my experiences* even more.

My professional career is drawing to a close, so I would like to share a little of the knowledge I've gathered along the way to help you become a more effective manager.

One of the things I've discovered is that you don't have to be the smartest person on your team to be a great manager; you just have to know how to lead people to "peak performance."

In "Managing to Peak Performance," I will share what I've learned while leading teams in a variety of different roles – starting as a teenager at Tunnelton High School and up until today, at age 60. I will share examples, both positive and negative, that I have experienced first-hand or have seen while observing other executives, managers and supervisors.

While I am very quick to acknowledge my favorite managers, co-workers and clients by name while sharing numerous positive examples of effective leadership, I am also extremely careful *not* to identify those who might have provided glaring examples of less-than-stellar management. The purpose of "Managing to Peak Performance" is *not* to criticize or embarrass any individual or organization, but to help others learn from what I've seen and experienced.

As I wrote, I was determined to *show* you – not just *tell* you. The reality is that you can seldom convince readers of anything by *telling* them, but if you can *show* them through personal anecdotes they can relate to, they will understand and may begin to change their way of thinking. By sharing stories based on my experiences as a manager and what I've seen while working with and consulting for so many different organizations in West Virginia and across the country, I hope to inspire you to become a more effective leader.

Let me *show* you how to become a manager who leads his or her team to improved performance, one that people actually *want* to follow. At the end of each chapter, I will share questions and activities that can guide you to achieve peak performance in your career and with your team.

The first three quarters of this book detail the *how* and *why* of my management philosophies, while in the last few chapters I dive a little deeper into my personal background – and why I have strived to inspire others during my career and life. I think you will find Chapters 23 and 24 particularly interesting and maybe even a little enlightening!

I hope you will enjoy reading more about my incredible personal journey, from surviving experimental open heart surgery in 1963 at age five and growing up in a small West Virginia community, to working with, leading and providing consulting services for dozens of America's most dynamic organizations.

Chapter 1: Showing vs. Telling

Now, they understood.

While working as Director of Media and Community Relations for North Carolina Power/Virginia Power (now known as Dominion Power) in the late 1980s, I talked with my manager, Jack Runion, about purchasing a fax modem that would have allowed me to send press releases to dozens of media outlets in our two-state service area automatically from my computer. The fax/modem would allow me to disseminate press releases while I could continue to work on my computer and respond to phone calls from the news media.

Jack was one of the best, most supportive managers I've had in my career, but we were nearing the end of the fiscal year and all departments were being directed to limit expenditures.

"How much is it?" Jack asked.

"It's about $400," I answered.

"I know our budgets are pretty tight right now, so let's look at this – maybe next year."

"OK, Jack."

I understood that we were in the middle of a budget crunch, but I also knew that this technology would allow me to work more efficiently.

A few weeks later, we were in the midst of hurricane season, which meant I would now be working numerous weekends and evenings. I had worked two full weeks and weekends in a row directing crisis communications during a minor hurricane and a tropical storm that hit the coast of North Carolina and moved up through that state and into our service area in southwestern Virginia. The two storms caused outages to thousands of customers, each lasting two or three days throughout a very wide area.

Now, a third storm was threatening to hit the coast – once more over the weekend.

"Just give me a call if you need my help," Jack said at the office as he left on a Friday afternoon for an economic development meeting. Jack was the type of leader who always offered to help me with anything, but also allowed me the freedom to do my job.

I called him that Sunday morning from our office, explaining that I had worked late Friday evening and all day Saturday, responding to media inquiries and faxing out restoration updates for the latest storm. I was drained after working nearly three weeks straight with extremely long hours, but I also wanted my manager to get a feel for just how difficult it was to perform this work without all of the tools needed to do it efficiently.

"I could use a little help, Jack," I said over the phone. "I'm faxing out press releases and answering reporters' questions. Can you give me a hand?"

"No problem, Randy. "I'll be right in."

He arrived at the office in less than an hour, although he lived a full half hour away from the office.

"What can I do?" he asked.

"While I'm calling reporters back, can you fax out the latest press release?"

"How do I fax it?" he questioned.

I handed him an eight-page list of all the media contacts throughout our service area in North Carolina and Virginia.

"Take this list and type in the first fax number on the machine," I explained to him. "Put the press release in the machine and hit 'send.' Then continue down the list for each number and do the same. That's all you have to do."

"No problem. I have to type in every number?" he asked with a look on his face that basically said, "Seriously???"

"Yes, every number."

While I returned reporters' calls, I heard the beeping sounds as Jack typed in each number and then the witch-like screech of the fax machine connecting with another machine somewhere in Virginia or North Carolina as the press release was sent electronically to the news media, one by one.

About 90 minutes later, Jack popped his head inside my office.

"I finished them all, but there has to be a better way of doing this," he said. "Just sending out the press release, one press release at a time, took nearly two hours."

"There is a better, easier way, Jack. Remember that fax/modem I talked with you about a few weeks ago."

"Yes?"

"Here's how it works. I can program this fax/modem to work in the background of my computer, automatically sending out the press release I've typed and formatted," I explained. "With one click of a button on my computer screen, I can send out the press release to all of the radio stations, newspapers and television stations you faxed today. I can even group the media list so that I can choose which areas to send the release. Plus, after it's done faxing, I receive a report to tell me if the press releases were transmitted successfully."

"That sounds like a great time saver in the long run," Jack said.

"It would be," I responded. "But it's about $400 and our budgets are tight."

"I don't care. It will be worth it," Jack said. "Order it tomorrow. I'll talk to the vice president about it. It's clear we need this, now that hurricane season has started. We *will* find the money."

I tried to *tell* Jack how much more efficiently I could complete my work with a computer fax modem, but it wasn't until I *showed* him how inefficiently we were working that he truly understood. I knew Jack would strongly advocate for us to purchase this equipment, if he only understood. Now he did.

This is an example of what I would call "managing up," by showing not telling.

△ △ △

A few years later, working with the same electric utility, I developed the concept for a high-tech summer camp to encourage more female and minority high school students to enter math, science and engineering fields. The program was called Tech High. (We originally started the program at Chowan College in Murfreesboro, North Carolina, but it was such an overwhelming success that the company expanded it to Virginia Commonwealth University, Longwood College and James Madison University.)

In addition to allowing students to utilize electron scanning microscopes, DNA staining kits, robotics and other high-tech tools at this week-long summer program, I wanted students to walk away from the camp with a much better understanding of the vital role power companies play in meeting the energy needs of consumers, while also balancing environmental and economic concerns.

Sure I could have *lectured* the students, but I wanted to *show* them. I wrote a tabletop simulation called "Energy, the Environment and Economics." My plan was to have teams of students work through 20 different activities or decisions. Each activity represented one year in the history of a fictionalized small country, with the goal of the game being to meet the present and future energy needs of consumers, while also creating jobs, generating tax dollars and protecting the environment. Each activity's decision "cost" a specific number of jobs, money, environment and energy points. After each team made its decision for each specific activity, a team member would turn the page of the game to determine the outcome.

Depending on the decision made, each team would gain or lose jobs, money, environment and energy points – sometimes gaining points in one category while losing points in another. After testing the game with a couple of teenage students who were babysitters of my sons, I felt very comfortable talking to my planning committee about playing the game at Tech High.

After looking at a very tight agenda for the camp, our planning committee scheduled the game for the first thing on a Friday morning, after the students had traveled to a nuclear power station the day before, arriving home after 11 p.m. It seemed to be the most appropriate time – after visiting the power station.

"Randy, I just want to warn you that these students will be tired," an educator friend on the committee, John Parker, warned me after we slotted the game into the camp's schedule. "Don't be disappointed if a few of the students fall asleep because they're getting back so late the evening before."

"I think we'll be fine," I told him.

"OK, but I warned you," he said.

He was evidently very worried that the game would "fall flat," especially with an exhausted group of rising 10th grade high school students playing it.

I have to admit I was a little apprehensive to lead this activity with such a large group when the Friday morning finally arrived. Would this activity be successful, or would the students fall asleep, as my educator friend had predicted?

Although the students were a little dreary-eyed when we started the activity, they were soon screaming with excitement as their teams' scores were written on a dry erase board at the conclusion of each activity. The game required nearly three full hours to play, but the students' enthusiasm didn't wane. If anything, the exhilaration grew throughout the morning, peaking at the end of the activity to a crescendo of students yelling, screaming and jumping up and down as the scores for the final activities were posted.

Following the game, I asked a series of questions. It was clear from the students' answers that not only had they *thoroughly* enjoyed the game, but they also had gained significant insight into the delicate balancing act among meeting energy needs, creating jobs, protecting the environment and generating tax revenue.

Later, I led the game with a group of graduate engineering students at James Madison University, with a similar reaction in both excitement and knowledge gained. In fact, the department head commented to me that his students learned more in three hours while playing this game than they would normally learn after six weeks of lectures. I provided him with a copy of the game and gave him permission to use it with all of his graduate students moving forward.

As you can now see, I was able to show students, high school and graduate school, the impacts of energy decisions, positive and negative. Instead of just being lectured, students were helped to understand key energy concepts, because they had the opportunity to make decisions that allowed them to truly learn.

△ △ △

Let me provide you with yet another example of showing vs. telling.

Because of my extensive experience in public relations and directing communications during numerous crises, I have trained hundreds of business and community leaders in America and even from locations around the world how to communicate effectively during emergencies. Most crisis communication training seminars consist of a three- or four-hour PowerPoint presentation with recorded "mock interviews" at the end of the training. Nearly every such seminar I have ever participated in or led during my career has followed the same lecture/practice/critique format.

I knew that I could do a much better job of teaching participants, if I could just *show* them the impact of crisis communications instead of just telling them through a PowerPoint presentation. Based on my experience directing communications for two school districts and the West Virginia Department of Education, I added a component to the training that allowed company managers to understand the importance of timely, effective crisis communications on a very personal basis. Here's how I did it.

On the first opportunity I had to test this new training component, I divided corporate plant managers into teams and provided them with the scenario that they are driving to work one day when they hear on the radio that a bus has collided with a semi-truck. They learn through a radio announcement that the accident occurred at a location where their sons or daughters would be riding a bus, and at a time when they would be on the bus to school.

The purpose behind this component of the training was to help participants put themselves in the shoes of those they would be communicating with through the news media during a crisis. When I asked the teams, "When would you like to know more information?" and "How often do you want updates?" they responded emphatically.

They wanted answers – NOW!

When I further queried the managers about what they needed and wanted to learn, managers responded that they wanted to know immediately which bus was involved, if students were injured, a phone number they could call for additional information, and if students were taken to the hospital. The managers wanted information quickly and more updates as additional information became available, they explained.

I could see the look of panic on their faces as they thought about their children potentially being on a bus struck by a semi-truck and then learning about this accident on a radio announcement on their way to work. They felt helpless and had to rely on receiving information from others to allay their deepest, darkest fears.

At the end of the discussion, I asked the managers how this scenario involving a bus accident was any different from an incident at one of their facilities, whether it was an environmental incident or an industrial accident. I explained to these leaders that the immediate stress and panic they felt as parents in this mock scenario is exactly what parents and family members in their communities would feel if they didn't know what had occurred at one of their facilities, if their families were in any danger, or if a beloved relative was injured or killed during an industrial accident.

The looks on their faces told me all that I needed to know. Now they understood.

This exercise was more powerful than the PowerPoint presentation alone – and it set the tone for the remainder of the training. Following this exercise, I could easily tell that the managers became very serious about learning how to communicate effectively during a crisis. They approached the training a lot more earnestly and asked more questions, realizing that communicating during a crisis is vitally important for their organizations as well as for community members affected. It also helped these leaders to understand how to become more effective, better and even more empathetic communicators during a crisis.

As I have managed, trained and consulted with people and organizations throughout my career, I have consistently remembered the importance of showing vs. telling. Instead of just telling people what to do and how to do it, I have always tried to lead others so they could see and feel the impact of their decisions – and take ownership for them.

Peak Performance Chapter Activities:

1) Do you tell your employees what to do, or do you spend more time showing them?
2) How can you show your employees what you want them to learn or see?
3) How can you show your employees the true impact their decisions have on clients or customers?

Chapter 2: Leading at an Early Age

After all, I thought, how could I ever convince them that we could win, if I didn't believe in them?

Forty-five years ago, while in my sophomore year at Tunnelton High School in West Virginia, I was asked by a classmate if I would take over as coach of his elementary intramural basketball team that played in an after-school league.

He explained to me that his team wasn't very talented and hadn't won even one game all season long. The season was about two-thirds over when he asked me to become the team's coach. My classmate practically *begged* me to take over leadership of his team. He was tired of losing. I reluctantly accepted, not knowing that this would become one of the best learning experiences of my life and would help to shape the way I would lead people during my career.

At our first game a couple days after taking over, I discovered why this team wasn't winning. On the surface, it appeared to be the least talented group of players in the entire league, players hadn't been taught many fundamentals and they didn't play at all like a team. Although there were only 12 teams in this after-school league, we were the worst – by far.

I don't remember all of the individual players on this team I coached 40+ years ago, but I do vividly recall a short, but very quick guard, Bruce, who loved to dribble and shoot the ball almost as soon as he reached the top of the arc; a forward, Pat, who was stocky and a little slower than other players getting up and down the court;

a quiet player named Bill other players seemingly ignored during the games; and a center, Jim, who was at least four inches shorter than other players at the same position in the league.

We lost the first game I coached by at least 16 points. I noticed immediately that the team actually *believed* it was going to lose – before the first jump ball to even start the game.

Seeing the self-defeating attitude and horrific performance of this team, I was determined to do two things as coach: 1) help players to believe in themselves, and 2) give them the best opportunity of winning.

I knew each of these goals would be very tough to achieve. I also knew that if we would ever have any chance of winning, I had to glean every ounce of ability out of these young players.

At practices held after school, I began teaching the team a basic 2-3 zone, and emphasized that when we were on defense, all players would raise their arms and hands to make it a little more difficult for the other team to pass. My thinking was that if we could create even two or three more turnovers a game, this would result in fewer scoring opportunities for the other team – and more chances for us to make baskets.

I also began coaching my players to never take a shot unless they were inside the foul line. We had to improve our shooting percentage dramatically and this was one way to do it – taking shots closer to the goal.

At every practice, we worked on the importance of passing to an open player, and we also drilled on all of the fundamentals, including dribbling, passing, rebounding and using the backboard when shooting near the basket. I knew that in order for us to have any chance of winning, we had to do more things right than the other teams in order to make our team a lot greater than the sum of its individual parts.

More important than practicing fundamentals, I also worked on helping these young players believe that they could win. I praised them when they did things during a game the same way we had practiced, and I emphasized just how close we were to actually winning – not just that we continued to lose. We celebrated each individual victory, no matter how small. A great pass was recognized, as was when a player remembered to use the backboard when shooting a layup. Slowly but surely, habits began to be imprinted on these young brains that improved our team's performance.

I began to change, too. I started seeing each player's individual talents as strengths I could utilize – not just thinking of them as players who may not have had the same level of talent as players on other teams in the league. After all, I thought, how could I ever convince them that we could win, if I didn't believe in them?

Bruce was the player I trusted to bring the ball up the court, because of his innate dribbling ability. I coached him at practice and in the remaining games to never take the first shot – that he was expected to pass the ball to another player once he dribbled to the foul line – if not before.

Pat, my stocky fifth grader, became my best rebounding forward and a great passer. He would position himself under the basket and his size allowed him to block out other players and rebound the ball.

Jim, our center, was expected to be the first player up and down the court on every possession, because of his high energy and speed – and also to compensate for Pat's lack of speed. Jim ran like a deer and almost always beat other taller, slower centers up and down the court on offense and defense.

I wish I could say that by the end of the season, we had won a couple of games, but we hadn't.

We lost every single one of our remaining games.

By the end of the season, though, we were losing to teams by three or four points that we had lost to earlier in the year by as many as 20. That was progress, and we celebrated it as a team.

That's not the end of the story, though.

With the regular season over, we now had a second chance in the post-season tournament. I emphasized to my players that we were now undefeated and in first place just like every other team in the league. We had a fresh start, as it was a brand new season – the post-season. Our first tournament game was scheduled against one of the top teams in the league.

Randy D. Shillingburg

I'm not sure how or why it happened then, but all of the coaching, all of the work on fundamentals, and all of the focus on playing as a team and not just as a group of individuals finally clicked in our first tournament game.

We won our first game of the entire year by six points!

Bill, the player completely ignored for most of the season by the rest of the team, was finally passed the ball – repeatedly. He scored 13 points in that initial tournament game, after probably not scoring 13 points all season long. Bruce did a masterful job dribbling the ball up the court and passing to open players. Pat was our leading rebounder and when Jim beat other centers down the court, Pat passed him the ball for a couple of easy layups. Although not great at everything, each player was great at one or two things. We finally put all of the parts together to play as a true team!

No team – high school, college or professional – has ever been more exhilarated after a win than my fourth, fifth and sixth grade players. We had finally broken through with a win after an entire season of losing. The smiles on those young boys' faces made all of our hard work worthwhile. Having tasted a little success, this team now believed it could win – against any team. You would have thought this team had won the Super Bowl!

We won two more games in that tournament, before losing in the championship game to the top-rated team by only three points. We were disappointed to lose, but we were also very proud of just how far we had come together. We nearly won the championship after not winning a single game the entire regular season!

I have never forgotten that group of young people as I have managed for and consulted with people and organizations all over America – from Los Angeles to Miami, Indianapolis, Connecticut, South Carolina, Montana, New York City and various places in between. That team taught me more about leading people than probably any management seminar I have attended. That group of fourth, fifth and sixth graders taught me to believe in the power of a group of individuals, all working together, with a coach or manager fully utilizing the talents of each member, to create a great team.

I learned as a sophomore in high school the importance of quality coaching – assembling the talents of each individual team member to make the whole so much greater than the sum of its parts – and then focusing on the fundamentals to achieve improved performance.

Imagine, though, if I had asked my forward, Pat, to bring the ball up the court. We probably would have lost the ball on nearly every possession!

Or what if I had I coached my small guard, Bruce, to establish position under the basket and become my main rebounder? He didn't have the height to out jump forwards and centers for the ball!

And what if I had asked Bill to be my other guard? Although an accurate shooter, Bill wouldn't have been quick enough to bring the ball up the court. We would have lost the ball on turnovers several times a game!

But what if I had benched Jim, my fast center, and replaced him with another player who may have been an inch or two taller, but didn't have the speed to run up and down the floor? We would have missed numerous layup opportunities that gave us easy baskets!

Isn't this what many organizations do, though – place employees in positions where they cannot succeed – or can't make the best use of their talents? Don't many organizations also tend to focus on what employees *can't* do well, instead of focusing on what they *can* do very well?

During my career, I have seen so many organizations misuse and even waste the vast talents they had at their disposal or become focused on and frustrated with their employees' shortcomings. Everyone won't be great at everything, but when you make the best, most efficient use of available talents, the results can be magical. This is effective management that helps to lead teams to improved performance.

What I learned with that team is that managing to peak performance is first and foremost an attitude, an attitude of believing in the power of a group of people, all working together toward the same goal. Managing a team requires seeing the tremendous talents on your team and not just each individual's limitations, as so many managers do when they lead.

This experience with an elementary team helped to shape the mindset that I've retained during my career – the attitude of striving to be a great coach.

A great coach teaches others to work together and makes the best use of available talents. Winning feels wonderful, but even more gratifying is watching others around you achieve greatness because of your leadership.

During my career, working with organizations of all sizes and in different market sectors, I have seen on numerous occasions how changes in leadership can result in *completely* different results for the exact same team. Teams that were lackadaisical or underperformed became top-performing teams with the only change being the person in charge. Conversely, I've also watched as the best teams in an organization would begin to falter as soon as a change in leadership was made.

I believe that managing a team is much like putting together a jigsaw puzzle. Each piece has a specific place. Sure, you can try to force a piece into a particular spot, but it never really fits, and you won't be able to complete the puzzle because the piece you forced into the wrong spot will be missing where it's supposed to be placed. The individual pieces do nothing by themselves, but when placed together in just the right way, the puzzle can reveal a beautiful picture.

This is the role of a manager – to put the pieces together in just the right way.

△ △ △

While living in North Carolina in the 1980s and 1990s, I had the opportunity to watch a lot of Atlantic Coast Conference (ACC) basketball. Every year, Coach Dean Smith had one of the best teams in the league at the University of North Carolina (UNC). I remember hearing a joke one day that really stuck with me:

Question: "Who's the only person that can hold Michael Jordan under 20 points a game?"

Answer: "Dean Smith."

While Smith's teams were always well-coached and he seemed to be able to mold talented young men from all backgrounds into great men and positive role models, I would argue that he was rarely able to coach his players to their peak performance. He was a great recruiter, seemingly always encouraging two or three of the top 10 players in the entire country to enroll at UNC every single year. Smith won two national championships, with dozens of ultra-talented players who would go on to enjoy tremendous success in the NBA.

MANAGING TO PEAK PERFORMANCE

In comparison, Jim Valvano at North Carolina State won a single national championship with a team that paled in comparison to any of Dean Smith's UNC teams – in terms of overall talent. But Valvano was able to coach this team and many others to achieve more than the sum of his players' individual talents, which is why I have always viewed Valvano a better basketball *coach* than Smith.

A wonderful, caring man and respected leader, Dean Smith developed quality young men who were very well-prepared for a career in professional basketball and life. Don't misunderstand what I am trying to say about Coach Smith – he *was* a *great* man and positive role model for the young men he coached.

But did he effectively lead his young men to take full advantage of their tremendous individual talents on the basketball court, while minimizing their weaknesses?

I think not – at least not as well as Jim Valvano.

Peak Performance Chapter Activities:

1) List all of your team members.
2) List their individual strengths.
3) List their individual weaknesses.
4) What roles are your team members best suited to play?
5) Are you fully utilizing their talents in those roles?
6) How can you manage your team so that you maximize each individual's strengths, while minimizing their weaknesses – to make your team greater than the sum of its parts?
7) How can you adjust roles and responsibilities to take advantage of your team's talents?

Chapter 3: Caring about Your Employees

The look on Danny's face was priceless. For the first time in his career, he was being treated like a true professional.

It was the Monday before Thanksgiving in 1984. I was working in my office in Roanoke Rapids, North Carolina, when our North Carolina Power/Virginia Power Southern Division Vice President, Jim Earwood, stopped by to see me.

"Randy, what are you doing here?" he asked.

"I'm getting a few things done before the holiday," I answered.

"When are you going back home to West Virginia?" he queried.

"I'm leaving Wednesday evening after work," I said.

"No, you're not. You're leaving today."

"Jim, I haven't accrued any vacation yet," I argued. "I just started in September. I won't accrue any vacation time until the first of the year. It's company policy."

"No, you're leaving today. Randy, how many nights and weekends have you worked because of hurricanes and storms?" he asked.

"Well, I've worked quite a few."

"It's settled. You're leaving here today. Get out of here and go home to your family!"

Jim's gesture meant so much to me, a 26-year-old employee in a new job in a new town. He showed me that he was in tune with my needs as a human being. To this day, I think of Jim as one of the greatest leaders I've ever had the pleasure of working with during my entire career. Jim created a sense of strong loyalty within his team and helped to lead the transformation of the worst performing division in the entire company into the top performing division in just a few short years.

I have always remembered the lesson I learned that day from my vice president: If you want to get the most out of your employees, you have to develop a relationship with them – and anticipate their needs.

△ △ △

Several years later, I noticed that the performance of one of my key managers was slipping. She was typically one of my top performers but seemed as though her mind was elsewhere. She started missing management teleconferences and important deadlines.

Since I had spent time getting to know her over the previous couple of years, I asked what was going on in her life that was affecting her performance. I knew something was wrong.

She confided in me that she was facing a family issue that required quite a bit of her time and attention at home. I told her to take whatever time she needed, and that I would do all that I could to cover for her, completing some of her work if necessary and reminding her about the most important meetings and deadlines. She thanked me for my concern and support, and a few weeks later, she returned to being one of the top performers in the organization.

A lesser manager, not taking the time to develop a relationship with this employee, might have put her on a plan of improvement or even terminated her employment. Having spent significant time each month with this employee over the previous two years, I knew something wasn't right in her life, and I did my best to support her.

△ △ △

While working as Director of Communications for Kanawha County Schools, the largest school system in West Virginia, I managed an employee, Danny Noel, who ran the system's inter-office and school-to-school mail system. After I have been on the job just a couple of weeks, I noticed that Danny was always working a half hour or so before his official starting time, because he wanted to ensure that mail was delivered to schools as quickly as possible in the mornings.

I called him into my office.

"Danny, I notice that you're here working early every single day. Just between us, you're making what I would call a 'deposit' into your account. If you ever need to make a 'withdrawal' of time, let me know. If you're OK with our managing your time this way, I will work with you so that you don't have to take personal leave every time you want an hour or two off. I know you'll get your work done. I truly appreciate your hard work and dedication to the job."

The look on Danny's face was priceless. For the first time in his career, he was being treated like the true professional he was.

Every month or so, Danny would come in my office to tell me that he was making a withdrawal from his account. Although I told him he didn't have to tell me why he was taking a little time off, Danny explained each time that he was leaving a few minutes early to watch his daughter play softball on her high school team.

During the two years I managed Danny, I know he deposited two or three hundred extra hours into his account because he was such a dedicated employee. During that same time, Danny withdrew maybe 20 hours from his account to see his daughter play softball. Whether or not I gave Danny an hour or two off, he was still going to get his work done by starting work early. But by managing him the way I did, Danny felt as though he was appreciated and recognized, which is what every employee needs from his or her immediate supervisor.

A couple of years later, after leaving the school system and moving to a position with the West Virginia Department of Education, I learned that Danny had passed away. I drove to the funeral home for the viewing and introduced myself to his grieving wife. Her face immediately widened into a huge smile, although her eyes were still filled with tears.

"You're Randy! You were Danny's boss, weren't you?" she asked.

"Yes, I was. I loved working with Danny. I am so sorry for your loss," I told her.

"Danny loved working with you. You will never know how much he enjoyed your letting him make a withdrawal from his account so he could see his daughter play softball. It meant so much to him. Thank you."

Now *my* eyes were filled with tears.

△ △ △

Also while working with Kanawha County Schools, I had the opportunity to experience leadership that clearly was not attentive to employees' needs.

On a cold and snowy day, I was contacted by our Director of Transportation, George Beckett, who called me at 4 a.m. to tell me that the decision had been made to close schools that day because of dangerous, slick roads. It was my job as Director of Communications to alert the news media that we were closing schools so that parents, students and teachers could be informed.

By the time I had faxed out a press release to all local news media and answered a few media calls from my home, it was probably 5:30 a.m. I decided to head into work, since by that time it would have been a waste of my time to try to sleep for a half hour or so. Central Office staff members were expected to be at work that day anyway.

I drove to the school system central office and worked the entire day. Mid-morning, we were informed that the school board would hold its regularly-scheduled meeting that evening, even though schools were closed. The school board meeting started at 7 p.m.

Randy D. Shillingburg

Believe it or not, at 11:30 p.m. school board members were discussing how much cheese should be on school pizza. I'm not kidding.

With my head in my hands, listening to these community leaders debate whether or not pizza in the school system had too much or too little cheese, I nearly cried. I was *that* exhausted and frustrated. I had been awake for 19 and one-half hours straight. My only time away from work that entire day was a quick lunch break and a short dinner at home with my family. I had given the school system nearly all I could possibly give it that particular day, and I was expected to be back at work very early the next morning. But here I was, listening to a debate at nearly midnight about the amount of cheese on pizza. After a minute or two, I raised my head, looked around the room and saw several other members of the school system's leadership team – most of whom had been working for more than 16 hours – with their heads in their hands or shaking their heads in utter disbelief.

The meeting finally concluded a few minutes before midnight.

This is an example of leaders who clearly did not understand their employees' work, their needs as human beings or even their role as school board members. I left Kanawha County Schools as quickly as I could find another, better job. Others did, too, in what was a mass exodus of talented, hard-working, dedicated people in the coming months.

There wasn't a single person on our leadership team who would have complained for even one second about working long hours to improve the quality of education in our system, as we did this every single day. But to perform our regular jobs all day long and then spend what felt like half the night listening to a useless debate about the amount of cheese on pizza was a little much.

Clearly, that's not how people should be managed.

△ △ △

Years later, while managing a call center for a small business as Director of Business Development, I noticed that one of my most dedicated employees, Lori Cole-Boyce, would always come into work early. She was supposed to begin her shift at 8 a.m., but typically arrived at 7:45 a.m. if not earlier.

I asked her, "Lori, would you like to work from 7:30 to 4:30?"

"Oh my goodness, Randy," she said with a huge smile across her face. "That would be wonderful. I live about a half hour from here, so this schedule would allow me to get home earlier in the evening in the winter, which means I won't have to drive in the snow in the dark! I hate driving in the dark when it's snowing."

△ △ △

During my career, I've found that although a raise is appreciated by all, what is *most* valued is having a leader who is in tune with his or her employees' needs.

I have tried to be attentive to my employees' needs, whether it was giving them the afternoon off after a late evening of work, allowing them to come in later the next day, or adjusting schedules to better suit their lives and personal needs.

Sadly, everyone doesn't manage this way.

While I was working with one organization as a manager years ago, a young, pregnant employee regularly worked in the evenings as part of her job. Not only did the executive she reported to require her to arrive at work the next morning at the regular starting time, but she also made her take personal leave if she had a doctor's appointment in the afternoon. Clearly, this was leadership that did not care at all about its employees.

This style of uncaring management literally disgusted me and angered everyone who worked in that office. Nearly the entire staff left for other positions within a period of only two years.

Bad managers don't care.

Good managers listen to their employees.

Great managers pay attention to their employees so they can *anticipate* their needs.

Peak Performance Chapter Activities:

1) List all of your team members.
2) Write two interesting facts about each of your employees – outside of work.
3) What types of things mean the most to your employees?
4) How can you demonstrate to each of your team members that you care about them as people – and not just as employees?
5) If you currently don't have the time to get to know your employees better, what can you eliminate from your schedule or your duties so you will?

Chapter 4: Micromanaging

My dad, in his own way, taught this young foreman how to become a better manager.

My father, Clarence "Mutt" Shillingburg, worked in the Laborer's Union most of his working life. He told me a story when I was a teenager that I have *always* remembered.

A World War II vet, my dad shows up to work one day and learns that he has a new, first-time foreman, a much younger man with significantly less experience than my father.

Five or six times a day, the new foreman stops by to see my dad and asks him a series of questions:

What are you doing?

Why are you doing *that* now?

What will you be doing next?

Why don't you do is *this* way?

Why don't you do *this* next?

My dad was hard at work before the foreman stopped by, but, faced with what seemed like an inquisition, my father stopped working and answered the young man's questions. My dad had to essentially explain *everything* he was doing to the foreman, who clearly did not yet know how to manage his employees.

After a few days of being bombarded by questions several times a day, my father told me that he said to himself, "This foreman wants to tell me what to do, when to do it and how to do it, so I'll just stop working as soon as I see this guy coming around. I'm tired of this. I'll just stop whatever I'm doing and wait for him to tell me what to do. If he wants to talk, I'll talk."

Sure enough, as soon as my dad saw the foreman coming towards him, he dropped whatever he was working on and sat down, waiting on the foreman's instructions and questions.

After a few days, the foreman realized that if he allowed my father to work without interruption, my dad would get his work done, but if he kept bothering him, my father got little accomplished. My dad, in his own way, taught this young foreman how to become a better manager.

△ △ △

While doing some work with one organization, I noticed that the executives would consistently hire talented, very dedicated managers. After a few months, though, the leaders would begin telling their managers and all employees what to do, when to do it and how to do it. After a while, the executives attempted to make every decision.

One of two things will happen when employees are micromanaged: either employees will become disillusioned with not being allowed to do their jobs and will find other employment, or their managers will become disheartened with employees when they quit showing initiative and wait to be told what to do. If you think about it, this is exactly what micromanagers *train* their employees to do – because every decision employees make is second-guessed.

Either outcome will result in extreme turnover, which is what this organization experienced year in and year out. I have seen this same phenomenon occur in a few organizations, from Fortune 500 companies to the smallest businesses.

△ △ △

If you're an executive, it's vitally important that everyone on your team understands who owns "decision rights" for every type of decision. For example, a manager working under you may have the right to make any decision that only affects his department, as long as he or she is not overspending his or her allotted budget. Or, in some cases, managers may have the right to approve purchases under a certain dollar amount, but must receive executive approval for purchases that exceed that amount.

Decision rights can also be assigned to another person or to a group of people – or can be given to a team with "veto power" retained by an executive or manager.

Consistently, I have seen that the best, most efficient organizations allow employees or teams of employees to make decisions, providing true "ownership" in the organization. Most decision rights in these top-performing organizations are *driven down* to employees, not *driven up* to management and executives.

When decision rights are not clearly assigned at every level of an organization, it's very easy for executives or managers to overstep their decision rights and take them away from others. This ensures with near 100% certainty that employees will quit thinking and lose the initiative to make decisions.

Delineating decision rights within an organization is an effective way to ensure that managers never become *micromanagers*.

Peak Performance Chapter Activities:

1) Have your employees lost initiative or seemingly have quit thinking?
2) Do you find that you or other managers are making nearly every decision?
3) If you answered yes to either of these questions, take some time to determine which decisions you and your managers are currently making that you should be able to trust your employees to make for your organization.
4) How can you drill more decision rights down to employees or teams of employees to encourage more "ownership" in your organization?

5) Facilitate a meeting with your managers to ensure that leadership in your organization understands who owns decisions rights for each type of decision.
6) Encourage managers to speak up loudly if you overstep their authority and take away their decision rights, or if they see an employee or manager stepping on your rights.

Chapter 5: Maximizing Sales Growth

My experience has been that many working in sales either think too big or too small.

One of the most challenging and rewarding positions in my career was growing a statewide office for a national organization, College Summit, from $85,000 to over $1 million in annual revenues in just three years in West Virginia, then managing sales executives for that same organization from Los Angeles to Miami and many locations in between. Sharing what I learned, which is detailed in this chapter, those teams across the country achieved 60%+ year over year growth in revenues even when our country was experiencing a deep recession.

I know a few of you reading this will say that this is "small potatoes," which it is. In a world of billion dollar businesses, growing an organization to over $1 million in revenues is a relatively small feat. But experiencing more than a 10-fold increase over a three-year period is impressive for any organization in any business or industry. I believe that what I learned about sales and revenue growth applies to *any* organization, from the smallest non-profit to the largest for-profit company.

Here's the most important thing I learned about managing customer relationships and how to grow revenues:

Focus near-equal amounts of time and attention among three groups of customers: 1) existing customers, 2) potential new customers, and 3) "flywheel customers."

Many sales people do an effective job of focusing their attention on potential new customers, seemingly always going after the "shiny new penny." The problem is that if sales people focus most of their attention on new customers, existing customers may soon feel neglected, which means that for every new customer they add to their portfolio they will probably lose an existing customer.

That's not progress.

Sales people who focus all of their attention on existing customers will never see strong revenue growth, because they will rarely add new customers. Their existing customers will appreciate the undivided attention, but sales growth will be very slow and limited to upsales.

Lastly, those in sales who focus all of their time, energy and resources on new and existing customers will never experience *significant* growth because they are spending all of their time and energy on single customers.

The third type of customer, the "flywheel customer," is a person or organization that can open doors to numerous other sales opportunities. This concept refers to the term used in the book by Jim Collins, "Good to Great." (The flywheel is a very heavy wheel that once you get moving gains momentum with each subsequent turn.) I view flywheel customers in this way – they can propel you forward very quickly. Once you gain momentum with flywheel customers, it becomes easier to keep the "wheel" turning to grow your organization very rapidly.

Examples of a flywheel customer would be a professional organization, if the customers you target are members of that profession. A single presentation before this professional group could potentially provide you with dozens of new customers. If you're selling a product or service to public schools, a single presentation before the state board of education or a meeting with a key member of the department of education could open doors to dozens of new customers in districts all across an entire state. Even if you're selling soft drinks, the concept of a flywheel customer also applies. A single presentation at the headquarters for a large restaurant chain could conceivably open the door to *hundreds* of new customers. By focusing time on flywheel customers, a sales team can transform an average performing company into a true market leader very quickly.

My experience has been that most working in sales either think too big or too small. Each singular focus has significant pitfalls.

By too big, I am referring to those who only set their sights on the flywheel customers, without also doing the arduous, day-to-day work of adding new customers and serving existing customers. These single customers help to get the flywheel turning by providing you and your organization with credibility. Sales people who focus most of their attention on flywheel customers are either a huge success, which is very unlikely, or a gigantic failure, which is much more probable. There never seems to be an in-between.

I once worked with a sales executive who focused almost all of his attention on flywheel customers, while ignoring existing, long-term customers. He was always looking for the one "big hit." Within one year, though, he had lost most of his existing, long-term customers, but was never able to sign a contract with even one flywheel customer. The office he managed closed just two years after he took over what was the most successful team in his organization. Ineffective sales leadership can tear apart an organization very quickly.

By "too small," I am referring to those sales people who only think in terms of single customers and are always working extremely hard, but are never truly successful. They aren't ambitious enough and rarely focus time or effort on those flywheel customers that can propel sales quickly and exponentially.

By focusing sufficient time, resources and effort on all three groups of customers, a salesperson will not only retain existing customers and add new customers consistently, expanding revenues each and every year, but will also drive increased revenues quickly through those flywheel customers.

This concept of investing time on all three types of customers also provides an organization with financial stability. By not focusing on any single group of customers, an organization's odds of *sustainable* success even during an economic downturn are much greater.

As the saying goes, never put all of your eggs in one basket.

Accept what I learned through dumb luck as a great gift – a lesson you won't have to learn through years of trial and error. Sales isn't rocket science, but I discovered that focusing on three, distinct groups of customers with near-equal attention leads to long-term, sustainable and even rapidly-growing sales growth.

Isn't that what we all strive for if we work in sales or lead sales teams?

△ △ △

I also learned a few other sales basics, while participating in and leading sales calls with various clients in West Virginia and all over the country in a wide variety of positions. Here are four key points I learned about sales, whether selling a product or service to a Fortune 500 company, one of the nation's largest school systems or even trying to raise funds from philanthropic partners for a non-profit organization:

Listen and learn
I learned that if I spent more time listening than talking I would often obtain key information I could use in my sales presentation – information that would be important to my potential customers and clients. By asking leading questions, I would be able to learn how my pitch might work best (and which words to use) when presenting to a particular client.

I remember one sales call in particular in Long Beach, California. One of my team members and I learned *exactly* what would be most meaningful to a particular potential client by asking a series of questions – and then closed an *immediate* sale totaling over $200,000 because we tailored our pitch *exactly* to our potential customer's needs.

Don't "ask" until you know the answer
Many salespeople make the "ask" too quickly, before taking time to develop a relationship. After developing a relationship with a particular customer or client, asking leading questions and doing *extensive* research about the organization, I would typically know with near 90% certainty what the answer would be if I asked for the sale.

I recall a sales meeting I had scheduled with the president of a regional bank several years ago. After the meeting, I called my boss, a vice president in our organization, who asked, "What was the 'ask?'"

I told him, "I didn't even make the 'ask.' This was our first meeting. I want to develop a stronger relationship and learn more before I ask for anything."

My vice president seemed a little surprised, but trusted me to follow up and complete the sale.

I developed the relationship over a couple of months and closed the deal. I didn't just want the quick sale. I wanted to build long-term, trusting relationships with my customers and clients!

Think of a business relationship involving sales like a courtship. You definitely wouldn't ask for a girl's hand in marriage until you know the answer will be "Yes!" and you shouldn't make the sales "ask" until you know with very high probability that the answer will be "Yes" in a business relationship.

"No" merely means "not yet"
Yes, I was infrequently turned down, typically early in the "courtship," before I would even make the official "ask." I might hear that an organization's budget was very tight or its focus wasn't in line with what I was selling. I learned to never take a "No" to mean "Never," but just "Not yet." I would estimate that probably 75 percent of the customers or clients who initially turned me down eventually said "Yes" because of my persistence as well as my continued efforts to keep them engaged in a meaningful way. Being a salesperson means you *will* be rejected. The best salespeople never give up and are more interested in developing relationships than making a sale.

While being involved in sales in nearly every market sector, I learned that if a salesperson focuses on the money he or she will struggle to secure the dollars, but if he or she focuses on the relationships and quits worrying about the money, the dollars will ultimately pour in. Being in sales is nothing more than developing and growing relationships!

People who worked with me in sales were always amazed at how few customers I lost from year to year. "How do you do this, Randy," they asked. My answer was always the same.

"I focus on developing long-term, mutually-beneficial relationships, and just not making the quick sale."

The importance of emotion and logic
The fourth point I learned about sales is the importance of using both emotion and logic to pitch products and services. By asking leading questions, you will be

able to understand whether emotion or logic is most important to your potential customers.

For many people, the emotional reasons why they should purchase are most important, while for others the logical, numbers side, may be vital. But even for those people driven largely by emotion, the numbers may be the deciding factor that will allow them to say, "Yes!"

For example, a person may absolutely *love* the feel, smell and design of a new automobile, but once he or she learns that the new car will result in savings of $100 per month in gas, the deal may be closed.

Even when pitching to a "numbers guy," never forget to devote at least a small portion of your pitch to his emotional side, and when attempting to sell to someone driven more by emotion, don't completely ignore the logical, numbers side of your sales pitch.

△ △ △

A few years ago, when I was first starting my consulting business, I coached a young man who had opened his own one-person business. His father, who was a friend, asked me to mentor his son. Although the 20-something had been in business just a few months, bankrolled by his father, he had not made a single sale. Within a couple months of my working with him, he had secured contracts totaling over $100,000! I coached him weekly, using all of the principles outlined in this chapter to help him grow his business very quickly – from developing an effective sales pitch to tailoring his messaging for both emotion and logic, and the importance of asking leading questions.

Working in sales is the toughest, most challenging position you will ever have. But if you begin to think about sales, not in terms of dollars and cents, but as the opportunity to build quality relationships over a period of time, your sales *will* come, and you will retain the same very satisfied customers every year.

The sales principles outlined in this chapter will produce results in any sales organization, no matter how big or how small – or what you're selling!

Peak Performance Chapter Activities:

1) Ask each of your employees to make a list of current customers or clients.
2) Ask your employees to write a list of clients or customers they are currently prospecting.
3) Ask your employees to break out the list of clients or customers they consider as flywheel customers.
4) Now, ask your employees to estimate how much time they spend with each group of customers – existing customers, potential new customers and flywheel customers.
5) Are your employees adequately balancing their time among the three groups of customers?
6) How can you ensure that your organization is balancing sales efforts to maximize revenue growth?
7) What training do you provide your sales people? How can this training be made more effective using the principles outlined in this chapter?
8) How can you train your employees to become more effective sales people by becoming better relationship builders?
9) How can you train or encourage employees to utilize pitches that appeal to the emotional and logical sides of your potential customers?

Chapter 6: Winning

The difference between a winning team and a losing team is almost always leadership, not the team members.

To me, winning is the ability to create a positive change in the direction of an organization or team. During my career, I have worked with dozens of winning teams and I have also led a large number of teams, transforming them from mediocrity (or worse) to become successful in their fields.

Sadly, I have also worked with a few leaders who have had the *uncanny* ability to convert once-winning teams into ones that struggled to survive or failed miserably. In one instance, I saw an executive transform what was once an organization's top-performing team into the worst in just two years with mean-spirited, self-focused leadership.

So, what's the difference between a winning team and one that consistently loses?

No matter where I have worked in the country – or what organization I worked with or consulted for – I have seen that the difference between a winning team and one that struggles is always leadership, not the team members. I have discovered over the past three decades-plus working with dozens of organizations in many different industries and market sectors that people who lead highly-successful teams always exhibit the exact same characteristics:

- An unwavering belief in the team and its ability to succeed
- An unwavering positive outlook

- The ability to communicate the complex by making it simple
- The ability to set high expectations and then communicate those expectations clearly to team members
- The ability to inspire

The few managers I have worked with who led unsuccessful teams displayed all or many of these attributes:

- A lack of belief and trust in team members
- A negative outlook (always looking for fault or where to place blame)
- The ability to make the simple very complex
- The ability to set low expectations or a failure to communicate expectations clearly
- The ability to instill fear and distrust among team members

The differences between people who lead winning teams and those who manage teams that consistently struggle are just as dramatic as the differences between their teams' performances.

Are you a manager who leads a winning team? Or is your team consistently underperforming?

Peak Performance Chapter Activities:

1) Rate yourself candidly on a scale from 1-10 (with 1 being very low and 10 being the highest possible level) in the following areas:
    - An unwavering belief in the team and its ability to succeed
    - An unwavering positive outlook
    - The ability to communicate the complex by making it simple
    - The ability to set high expectations and then communicate those expectations clearly to team members
    - The ability to inspire
2) Now ask your managers or employees to rate you in these same categories. Ensure that they can rate you anonymously and without repercussions.
3) Compare how you rated yourself to how your employees rated you.
4) Why do you think how you rated yourself and how your employees rated you is different in some areas?

5) In which areas do you need improvement?
6) In which areas are you strong?
7) How can you transform yourself to become a "winning" leader?

Chapter 7: Testing Management Philosophies

The other manager focused on finding employees doing something wrong. I focused on finding employees doing something right.

When I moved back to West Virginia in the mid-90s, I was offered the unique opportunity of leading large groups of managers and employees in a production environment – a brand new customer service center with l companies and other major corporations as clients. When I accepted the job, I was searching for a chance to start rebuilding my career after a downsizing and moving back to my home state. Little did I know that this would become probably the most insightful management experience of entire my professional career.

The center employed 240 employees at its peak, with two shift managers, each managing half of the floor, and a total of 12 managers working under them.

I was one of two shift managers. The other manager had extensive experience in this field. She had six managers working under her, five of whom had extensive experience working in the telemarketing field. Her side of the floor employed 120 people.

Six managers were working under me, too, five of whom had no experience whatsoever in this field. My side of the floor employed 120 people, too.

Within two months of the facility's opening, though, my half of the floor and its employees were outperforming her side of the floor nearly every single day.

How was this even possible, given my relative inexperience, as well as my managers' lack of experience in the field?

Several months earlier, I had participated in Covey Leadership Training with North Carolina Power/Virginia Power. Based on this training, still fresh in my mind, as well as my previous leadership experiences, I tested my management philosophies in this very tough, results-based production environment. I couldn't have selected a better laboratory to test my theories about how to lead people most effectively.

I led much differently than the other shift manager.

The other shift manager focused on finding employees doing something wrong. I focused on finding employees doing something right.

She managed with fear and intimidation. I led with enthusiasm and positive reinforcement.

When company executives visited our facility, the other shift manager sequestered them behind closed doors, keeping them entirely to herself. When executives visited our facility and met with me, I walked them around the floor, praising my managers for their leadership and our employees for their great work.

The other shift manager watched her computer screen all day, rarely standing up from her desk, except to go to lunch. I paid attention to computer reports, too, but I also spent a large portion of my day walking the floor, working with my managers and encouraging employees.

Let me provide you with an example of just how different our management styles truly were.

On a Saturday while I was overseeing the entire floor, an employee, the employee's aunt (who also worked there) and one of my managers came rushing up to my work station. The two ladies were both hard-working, dedicated employees who rarely missed any time. I saw the look of panic on their eyes as they approached my desk. They blurted out that the mother of one of them had suffered a heart attack and was being rushed to the hospital.

"Get out of here and go to the hospital!" I told them.

On Monday, the employees were back to work, as their family member was stabilized and recovering nicely from what turned out to be a very minor heart attack. They were told by our human resources representative and even the other shift manager (who was in the human resources office at the time) that they would need to bring a note from the doctor *proving* that their family member had suffered a heart attack so that they wouldn't be charged for unscheduled time off.

"Don't worry about it," I told the employees when they came to talk with me. "My managers and I keep track of your time. That was definitely an excused absence."

The difference in management styles was very clear in the outcomes of our two sides of the floor. Even the company's top executives were amazed at how much better the employees on my side of the floor were performing than the other shift manager's.

Perhaps to assess if the results were due to my leadership style or the quality of my employees, executive leadership transferred the other shift manager to another facility and moved me to the other side of the floor, while assigning another manager to what was formerly my side of the facility. Within two weeks, my new side of the floor (which was previously the other manager's side) was now outperforming the other side (with my previous employees) nearly every single day.

While leading in this fast-paced environment with so many employees was challenging, it was also one of the best management experiences of my life. It taught me that no matter what the industry or business, quality management is the difference.

To paraphrase the great Wayne Dyer, what you will focus your energy on, you will receive more of – positive or negative. I focused on the positive in people and I received positive performance. The other manager focused on the negative and was always receiving less-than-stellar performance from her team.

No matter where I have worked, I have seen that managers who focus on the positive in their employees will lead teams that consistently outperform managers who consistently search for problems.

Peak Performance Chapter Activities:

1) How much time do you spend each day finding problems and affixing blame?
2) How much time do you spend recognizing employees' achievements?
3) If you're focusing more time on #1 than #2, then you're focusing on problems, which will only encourage more problems.
4) Purposefully begin to find people doing things right every single day, which will encourage stronger performance from your employees.

Chapter 8: Developing Employees

Manage people as though you want them to be working with you five years from now.

From 2004-2007, I worked for a non-profit, social entrepreneurial organization, College Summit, in West Virginia, helping it grow from $85,000 in revenues to over $1 million in those three years. From 2007-2011, I shared learned building and growing this office – which was this national non-profit's most successful team – with other teams across the country as Managing Director of Site Operations, providing executive oversight to teams all over America.

I was actually the second employee hired at College Summit in West Virginia. Forrest Wilder, our very talented Program Director, was already diligently at work when I arrived, starting the heavy lifting of changing the college-going culture in the Mountain State. I first served as Development Director, leading efforts to generate revenues that allowed our operations to grow, before being named Executive Director, after about a year with College Summit.

I first joined Forrest in an office loaned to us by our corporate champion, ECA, before moving the rapidly-growing team to an office in downtown Charleston, West Virginia, and finally to the campus of West Virginia State University. Forrest was a transfer from our national headquarters in Washington, D.C., with the goal of opening our West Virginia office. He fit right in because of his strong rural roots, growing up in Alaska. Everyone we worked with in West Virginia loved Forrest and appreciated his strong commitment to making a positive change in our public schools.

Randy D. Shillingburg

Forrest and I made a great team, as he provided quality programmatic support to our schools, and much-needed guidance to me, a new employee. He also had a work ethic second to none and always displayed unquestioned integrity. Forrest helped me to become acclimated into the College Summit culture, which was essential in order for us to grow a successful organization in West Virginia. Although he was probably 25 years my junior, I learned a lot from this very talented, dedicated young man. I have to say that whatever success College Summit had in West Virginia in subsequent years was due in large part to the strong foundation of quality work performed by Forrest before he moved back to D.C.

My previous experience working throughout the state – with schools and businesses in non-profit, for-profit and in two public education leadership positions – allowed me to hit the ground running in both selling our services to public schools and in raising philanthropy from corporations and foundations. As much as I might have been prepared for this unique role, I would not have been able to raise the revenues required to grow our organization without the help of two key people.

Pamela Scaggs, an old friend and co-worker at The Education Alliance, helped me to identify potential corporate and foundation grant opportunities – and taught me the importance of relationship-building in the world of sales. Everything I ever learned about development and sales, I learned from Pam. When Pam and I worked at The Education Alliance together, we were an unstoppable team, often attending meetings together not only to raise more funds for this statewide non-profit, but to also forge stronger connections with businesses throughout West Virginia. Pam was working with another organization when I began work with College Summit, but she enthusiastically shared ideas and grant opportunities that helped me to hit the ground running and to start generating needed revenues almost immediately.

Salli Gaddini, who headed up College Summit's grants department, helped me to become further acclimated into the organization's culture, while ensuring that all of our written proposals were well-crafted and clearly communicated the vital need for our work in West Virginia. While at College Summit, Salli took dozens of young people "under her wing." Although I was a lot older than most of the organization's employees, Salli became one of my key mentors. To this day, I consider Salli to be a very special person, a talented, insightful woman who helped dozens become successful at College Summit and grow as professionals, which assisted them in furthering their careers.

Of all the places I've worked in the past 37 years, College Summit was my favorite – by far. It truly was a "different" organization with very talented, dynamic, forward-thinking people leading it and working in offices all over the nation. The organization's three founders – J.B. Schramm, Derek Canty and Keith Frome – were the most innovative, passionate and intelligent people I've worked with during my entire career. I feel truly blessed to have been able to work alongside these three great leaders for seven wonderful years and to learn so much from each of them.

I would be remiss if I didn't also mention Brian Gaines, whom I reported to for most of my seven years at College Summit. The truth is that I have never enjoyed working with anyone as much as I enjoyed working with Brian. He was not only a wonderful mentor, but also a great friend. Brian has this "aura" of joy for life and people that inspires everyone around him.

Before I share more about my management philosophies while working with this life-changing organization, allow me to tell you a little more about College Summit – what it was trying to accomplish and how it was truly "leading-edge" in the non-profit arena.

College Summit's "Proof Plan" of sustainability (business plan) relied on two revenue streams – philanthropy and school sales. This organization's business plan relied on philanthropic dollars to fund fixed costs such as office and basic staff salaries, but then raised funds from school sales to offset the variable costs of serving additional students.

Although College Summit was a non-profit organization, school districts actually had to pay for our services, which ensured that schools had to be strongly committed to our program. We believed that schools needed to have "skin in the game," investing limited education dollars to implement our system of helping more low-income students transition to college.

In a nutshell, College Summit "supercharged" schools' guidance programs with students trained to guide other seniors through the process of enrolling and finding money for college, teachers trained to help students through the college transition process, a college transition curriculum and even online tracking tools that teachers and counselors utilized to ensure all seniors were receiving the help they needed in order to transition to education and training after high school.

In comparison, most non-College Summit schools had one overworked guidance counselor *attempting* to help guide 250 or more seniors during their transition to life after high school, while also counseling several dozen other high school students who might be facing emotional, disciplinary or family issues.

College Summit relied on contributions *and* sales revenues, so it clearly was an organization on the cutting edge – operating as a non-profit, but relying on revenues generated from school sales to sustain and grow its operations. Having worked in both for-profit and non-profit organizations, as well as two different public school systems and the West Virginia Department of Education by that time, I was innately drawn to what College Summit was attempting to do and the positive change it was making in high schools all over America.

According to the organization's business plan, when a College Summit office reached "scale" of 3,000 students served and $500,000 in philanthropy raised annually, it wasn't required to raise additional funds from contributors, because revenues from schools to serve each additional student would offset the "variable costs" of serving that additional student.

△ △ △

I am very proud that our team in West Virginia was the first in the entire organization to prove College Summit's business plan and reach "scale." We were the first office to prove this innovative business model – in one of the nation's poorest, most rural states.

The team we built in the Mountain State was one of the most dynamic, cohesive groups of people I've ever worked with during my career. I thoroughly enjoyed working with and then leading this team of dedicated people, and sincerely appreciated each team member's vital contribution to making a positive difference in the lives of so many West Virginians.

So, how did I manage this team?

If there was a single principle I followed while leading this wonderful group of people it was this:

I managed my team as though I wanted them to be working with me five or 10 years later.
What does this even mean?

It meant that during the latter part of my career I believe I had finally evolved into what Jim Collins would call a "Level 5 Leader." Instead of worrying about the present, I took a longer-term approach to organizational sustainability. It also meant that I was more concerned about helping my own employees grow as professionals than advancing my own career.

You see, when you manage people as though you *want* them to be working with you five years down the road, you invest the time to share what you've learned so that *they* can learn. You provide your employees with opportunities to lead and grow, which is what I strived to do with my College Summit team and many other teams I've managed. While this approach may feel a little frightening at first to many managers, once you make the transformation to worry more about your employees' development than your own career, you feel this tremendous weight being lifted off of your shoulders.

It's not about *you* anymore; it's about *them*.

I remember being at two key points earlier in my career and having managers working above me who were reluctant to promote me or to provide me with other opportunities within the same organizations. In one company, I was actually performing the job for which I was hoping to be promoted to, but my new boss was determined that since it took him 30 years to become a manager, I had to wait decades for my turn, too. The second instance was when I practically begged my boss for other opportunities to grow within the same organization, but was told that he didn't want to train someone else to do my job – because I was doing such a great job. Imagine that – being held back from other, more challenging and career-advancing opportunities, because I was doing too good of a job in my current role!

But I also fondly recall one of my first managers, Nancy Smithson, at Monongahela Power Company. She hired me a few months after graduating from college and trained me to be how to be public relations professional. After she left the Fairmont-based utility, she joined North Carolina Power/Virginia Power, working in its Richmond, Virginia, corporate headquarters. I contacted her several months after she left Monongahela Power, asking for a letter of reference. She provided me with a glowing recommendation, but also informed me about a job opening in the company's Southern Division Office, advocated for me and helped me join the company as Director of Media and Community Relations in Roanoke Rapids, North Carolina.

After those experiences early on – positive and negative – I decided that I would always advocate for my top employees when they were ready for the next steps in their careers. I also began using my role as manager to create opportunities that would provide my employees with the chance to shine as professionals. My experiencing the impact of having two managers who wouldn't advocate for me earlier in my career, and one who did, shaped who I became as a manager.

Let me show you just how different it is to lead in this manner.

As we were the first team in the organization to reach "scale" in 2007, outpacing other College Summit teams in major cities across the country to this prestigious honor, we planned a major press conference to celebrate. At that point, we were raising $500,000 through grants and donations and over $500,000 from school district sales, while serving over 3,000 West Virginia seniors, which was over one-sixth of all seniors in the state.

To mark this achievement, we invited our organization's CEO at the time, Dean Furbish, as well as the Governor of West Virginia, Joe Manchin. We planned the press conference at the Capitol in the Governor's Press Room, and invited a large number of dignitaries, including our local Board of Directors, as well as key school and business partners throughout the state.

When we started talking about planning the event, members of the team asked me what we were going to do and how I was going to lead the press conference. After all, I was the one with the public relations background. I surprised them with my reply.

"I'm not going to lead the press conference. You are."

I explained to our Operations Associate, Jayme Welbeck, and our Development Associate, Susan Shew, that *they* would be leading the press conference. They looked at me as though I had grown a full head of hair overnight (I am bald). I was asking two of our younger employees to lead a very important event for our team!

As these team members designed the program over the next several weeks, I helped to guide them a little using my previous experience, but they planned and then led the press conference. I may have asked a few leading questions to guide them to the right answers, but this was *their* event. Jayme kicked it off and turned it over to Susan, who introduced our CEO, who then introduced the Governor. Jayme ended the press conference with a few remarks.

They did a phenomenal job!

I never said a word or did anything during the entire press conference other than raising my hand when I was recognized by Jayme – and I was the executive ultimately in charge of this very successful team. I was proud of our entire team, not only for this achievement, but also for planning and executing the press conference to perfection!

Five, 10 and even 20 years in the future, I wanted these employees and our entire team to look back on this event with great pride. I wanted them to learn how to plan and lead a press event in order to be prepared for opportunities yet to come. I wanted them to have this experience because I knew I wouldn't always be around to lead them. I had already led numerous press conferences and helped to plan major events in my previous roles.

That was *my* time, though. This was *theirs*.

△ △ △

Let me share an example of what I would call egotistical, "me first" leadership.

While working in management for a very large organization with several hundred employees, I was asked to prepare a press release, which I emailed to the chief executive officer for approval.

I received a call from his secretary a few minutes later, asking me to come to the executive's office.

"Randy, this press release is wrong," he said. "Did someone not tell you the format that *they* prefer?"

"No, they didn't," I responded.

"Well, *they* want my name in the first paragraph of every press release that is distributed from our organization. That's the way *they* want it."

I noticed that he kept emphasizing the word, "they," but what he apparently meant was that *he* wanted his name in the first paragraph of every press release.

Randy D. Shillingburg

Although I had probably written 5,000 releases by that time in my career for at least a half dozen different organizations, I had never experienced working with an executive who wanted his name in the first sentence of *every* press release.

Clearly, it was never about his employees, the organization or its work. That day and every day it was *always* about *him*.

Let me share another, much more positive example.

While working with Kanawha County Schools as Director of Communications, Superintendent Jorea Maple recognized me for our "TeamWorks" monthly publication that was mailed to key community leaders and all employees. She praised me in front of nearly all the central office employees at a staff event and asked me to stand.

I stood up and thanked her for her kind words, but instead of taking credit for the publication, I motioned for my desktop publisher Karen Taylor, and our department secretary, Pat Hunter, to stand up. In front of the entire staff, I explained that these two employees deserved the credit for putting together this wonderful publication every month. I praised them in front of everyone and thanked them for their great work. Their faces beamed with pride as I recognized them in front of their peers!

I am amazed at how many managers cling to glory like a dryer sheet on warm clothes and are afraid to publicly praise employees for their contributions. My mindset of being a coach allowed me to feel great pride in seeing my team "win" without the need to even be recognized. Being an effective manager isn't about the recognition; it's about the gratification of seeing your team be successful and watching your team members bask in the glory.

I'm also stunned at a few managers who are reluctant to share what they've learned because one of their employees might advance farther up the organizational chart than they did. I'm astounded at how many managers actually limit the development of their employees, never giving them a chance to shine or to grow.

If you want to make your organization better and stronger, don't you *need* for employees to grow professionally, too?

△ △ △

After we had reached "scale" and our College Summit operations in West Virginia were sustainable and growing, I strongly advocated for Craig Grooms, our Program Director who replaced Forrest, to assume my role as Executive Director. I felt he was fully prepared for this next opportunity. I was actually ready to leave the organization so that he and my other valued employees would have the chance for promotions within College Summit. I had begun searching for other job opportunities outside of this great organization.

Rather than see me leave College Summit, Brian Gaines moved me to the position of Managing Director of Site Operations, which opened up advancement opportunities for members of the West Virginia team.

It wasn't about me anymore; it was about *them*.

I watched with great pride over the next couple of years as this team of very committed people served *more* West Virginia students and raised even *more* revenues through school sales.

△ △ △

I've been disillusioned when I have seen a few managers complain about a great employee who is five minutes late because of a major traffic accident on the interstate or when a personal or family issue causes that same employee to miss a couple days of work. My attitude has been that if you care about your employees – if you want to manage them as though you *want* them to be working with you five years from now – you will look past today to see what they can become tomorrow. With the proper, long-term mindset from their managers, talented, dedicated employees will pay back whatever time they miss 10-fold!

When you begin treating your employees as your organization's most essential assets, you will become a more effective leader. In doing so, you will quit worrying about your own career and begin focusing on *their* professional and personal growth, because they will drive your organization forward now and in the future.

Peak Performance Chapter Activities:

1) List all of your employees.
2) Beside each name, describe how you would manage each employee differently if he or she were still working with your organization five or 10 years from now.
3) What roles are your employees playing in your organization in the future?
4) Begin doing more of #2.
5) If you were to quit worrying about your own career and only about developing your employees to become the best they could be, what would you quit doing? What would you begin doing more?
6) Stop worrying about your own career and begin searching for opportunities to help your employees grow personally and professionally.

Chapter 9: Keep It Simple, Stupid

Focus areas for anyone you manage should always be very simple and easy to understand.

While working as Director of Media and Community Relations for North Carolina Power/Virginia Power and speaking with customers regularly through the news media, I had to communicate the complex by making it simple.

When explaining why a power outage occurred, I couldn't use the complicated engineering and construction jargon managers shared with me to explain why customers had lost power. I had to communicate in simple terms that customers could understand. Instead of talking about "reclosers" and providing a five-minute explanation for their use, I would use simpler words and phrases such as "Our safety equipment operated as designed to isolate the outage."

Let me show you another example of the importance of clear, effective communications using an even easier-to-understand example.

While in college, a friend was asked what sun glasses with polarizing lenses do. She tried to explain for probably three minutes about the direction of light rays and how polarizing filters reflect and refract light. This resulted in a *completely* confused look on the face of the person asking the question.

I explained what polarizing lenses do in a much easier-to-understand and clearer way.

"They cut down on the glare," I said, which resulted in an understanding nod from the person asking the question.

Today, doing consulting work for a wide variety of businesses, I have to accomplish the same goal – make the complex very simple. I pride myself on learning about businesses and then communicating what they do in a manner that the average customer can understand and appreciate.

Recently, I was asked by one of my favorite clients, Advanced Heating & Cooling, to help customers understand the energy efficiency difference between a single stage furnace and one that has a modulating gas valve. Sounds complicated already, doesn't it? Well, it's actually very simple if you explain it in a way that people can understand.

A single stage gas furnace is either all the way on or all the way off. It's like a car that can only be driven with the gas pedal all the way to the floor, or with the pedal not pushed down at all and the ignition switch turned off. Imagine how much gasoline you would use if you had to drive your vehicle on a long trip with the pedal all the way to the floor or your foot completely off the gas – with no in between!

In comparison, a furnace with a modulating gas valve can adjust the amount of natural gas being used, depending on the heating needs of the home, which makes it like the typical vehicle that allows you to push the gas pedal down a little of the way, or all the way down, depending on how fast you want to travel and what the terrain and road conditions might require. This is so much more efficient!

Pretty easy to understand, isn't it?

I've always had this knack for communicating the complex by making it very simple.

I first heard of KISS (Keep It Simple, Stupid) while attending a journalism workshop at Ohio University in the late 1970s. The elderly instructor brought a young lady up to the front of the class and kissed her innocently on the cheek. He said remember this: "KISS. Keep it simple, stupid."

I have always remembered the importance of keeping things simple for my employees.

△ △ △

While leading marketing and business development efforts as Director of Business Development for a small business a few years ago, I was asked to head up its call center, too.

When I started leading the call center, the "conversion rate" for the center was in the mid 80-percent range. The conversion rate was the percentage of customer calls that were actually being converted into sales appointments. This is vital data for any small business to know and measure.

Within a couple days of managing the center, I noticed three things: 1) The phone wasn't being answered quickly or consistently, 2) Customers weren't always addressed as pleasantly as I would have liked, and 3) Appointments weren't being booked quickly, which resulted in a few interested customers each week hanging up after being put on hold for several minutes.

To address how slowly the phone was being answered, I implemented a new system of answering customer calls, with the help of my call center team, of course.

The receptionist was asked to answer the phone before the end of the first ring.

If the receptionist were on the phone or unavailable, other customer service representatives were asked to answer the phone by the end of the second ring.

If the receptionist and the customer service representatives were on other lines or unavailable, selected office staff were asked to answer the phone before the end of the third ring. The idea behind our plan was that the overwhelming majority of customers would have their calls answered before the end of the first ring, with a few customers having to wait for two rings – but no customer would *ever* have to wait more than three rings!

By answering the phone quickly, our message to customers was very simple:

We appreciate your call and we want your business!

Isn't that the exact message you want to send to all of your customers if you're in business?

To address the second issue, I wrote a pleasant welcoming script for the receptionist and asked the receptionist and customer service representatives to envision that they were talking with their favorite grandmother, aunt, uncle, parent or other beloved family member whenever they were talking to customers. So, instead of just talking to some stranger, I wanted them to begin treating the customer on the phone as their favorite "Aunt Molly" or "Grandma Barb."

The pleasant, enthusiastic introduction by the receptionist and the manner in which our reps now communicated with potential customers projected strong messages on every single call about the type of company we strived to be – one that truly cared about its customers.

Addressing the third issue was more difficult and time-consuming. The calendar/booking system used by the company was and occasionally caused longer-than-wanted customer wait times. Customer service representatives would need to search several calendar pages, remembering times and locations to book appointments for customers that would allow them to group appointments geographically for our salespeople. Using this system, our representatives would often and very easily make mistakes, booking one appointment in a community one day, but completely missing that they had an open appointment in the exact same area a day or two earlier. By booking appointments in the same geographic area on the same day, our customer service representatives could reduce travel time and mileage for our salespeople.

To assist our customer service representatives in booking appointments more efficiently, I would search the calendar three or four times each day, looking for open time slots for salespeople, noting available appointment times in geographically-grouped appointments. I would type a sheet three or four times every day with available appointment times in specific geographic areas. I would provide this sheet to each of the customer service reps and other office staff members who were booking appointments. So, instead of searching multiple pages, our staff would look at the sheet I had created and inform a customer that an appointment was available in the customer's area at x a.m. on x day, turning a five- or 10-minute process of booking an appointment into one that required no more than a minute or two. As appointments were booked, representatives would communicate with each other about the time slots they had scheduled so that these appointment times could be marked off of their sheet, until I could provide them with an updated version.

Instead of having every person booking an appointment frantically search for several minutes for just the right time slot while a customer was on the phone, I performed this function for them, saving time and ensuring that appointments could be booked within a minute or two, instead of taking several minutes with a customer patiently (or not so patiently) waiting on hold.

Within just a few days after implementing our new system, the call center conversion rate in the mid-80s jumped into the low 90% range. This simple change can result in a *dramatic* improvement in revenues for a small company. I shared the positive results with my team and bought them lunch to demonstrate my appreciation for their hard work!

Let me show how much of an impact this seemingly minor improvement can have on any company's bottom line.

A typical week at a company with 100 "leads" (customers interested in having an in-home appointment) would result in 92 or 93 appointments being scheduled – compared to the 85 or 86 scheduled previously. With an average dollar per appointment generated through sales of even just $500, this would equate to an additional $3,500 to $4,000 in revenue each week for a company as a result of the call center's more efficient, more effective work. I don't know of any small business that couldn't use an additional $3,500 to $4,000 in weekly revenues!

The customer service reps appreciated and embraced this new, very simple approach. They proudly placed a sheet on their phones with our three focus areas printed in what amounted to short code that would help them to remember: 1) Answer the phone, 2) Talk to your grandmother, 3) Book appointments quickly.

Focus areas for anyone you manage should always be very simple and easy to understand.

Randy D. Shillingburg

△ △ △

During my travels now for Shillingburg Consulting, I frequent many of the same restaurants for coffee, breakfast or lunch. At one fast food restaurant in Morgantown, West Virginia, I visit every couple of weeks, it seems as if employees are *always* talking with one another or playing on their phones. What they *aren't* doing is quickly waiting on customers. I've waited in line five minutes or more before employees or a manager took time away from their personal conversations or phones to wait on other customers and me.

Just this past week, I stopped by for coffee and a breakfast sandwich. The young man at the front counter playing with his phone didn't wait on me or the person in front of me, but a young lady who moved about the speed of a badly-injured turtle finally waited on both of us after we had both been waiting at least two minutes.

After the person in front of me placed his order, I approached the counter and cheerfully said, "Good morning!"

The young lady said nothing.

I then told her what I wanted to order – a sandwich and a large coffee, even though she never even asked what I wanted.

She said nothing.

I inserted my debit card and after the transaction had been completed, she handed me the receipt – again without saying even a single word. The only words I heard her mumble was my order number, which she called out to let me know my food and drink were ready.

In comparison, the employees at a Burger King I visit often in Bridgeport, West Virginia, greet me by name. If for some reason the person designated to wait on customers is away from the counter for even a moment (i.e., collecting trays or cleaning the glass on one of the windows) when a customer enters the restaurant, you hear "Someone's at the front!!" announcement from two or three employees, almost in unison. This restaurant is very well-managed and treats its customers more like friends. This restaurant's management understands that the first and most important step in the sales process is waiting on customers!

Employees at this Burger King have taken the time to learn my name, so I have returned the favor, learning the names of those I see regularly. Just as they welcome me with my first name and a smile, I greet Jeff, Sherry, Chris, Shelby, Jonie, Gwen, Bree, Nancy, Courtney, Khristin and a few others with a big smile as I say their first names!

How many restaurants today don't make "waiting quickly on customers" their number one priority? Isn't that the very first step in providing customers with quality service?

How many restaurants today don't even attempt to learn their regular customers' names? Isn't that vitally important, too, if you want to show your regulars how much you appreciate their business and want them to come back?

△ △ △

Remember my elementary basketball team? My main focus areas with them were also very simple: 1) Don't shoot until you're inside the foul line, and 2) Put your hands up on defense.

For my center, Jim, his third focus area was to be the first person up and down the floor – on offense and defense – no matter what. For my guard, Bruce, his third focus area was to pass the ball at least once before *ever* shooting. For my forward, Pat, his third focus area was to box out and rebound – on every possession. Whenever my players did in the games what we practiced, I praised them, because it reinforced what I was trying to teach them.

The worst leaders I've worked with or have done consulting work for are those who have the seemingly uncanny ability to make the simple extremely complex, completely confusing everyone they manage.

Whether working with or consulting for a Fortune 500 company, government agency, non-profit organization or small business, I can always tell a lot about how effectively a person can manage based on how well he or she communicates the extremely complex by making it very simple and easy-to-understand.

Keep it simple, stupid.

Peak Performance Chapter Activities:

1) If you had to narrow down what you expect from everyone in your organization or on your team into three key points, what would they be?
2) Communicate these three points consistently and often.
3) Remind employees of these focus areas with signage and other regular reminders.
4) Reward and recognize employees for their great work and commitment to the focus areas.

Chapter 10: Putting Employees First

If employees you manage can't or won't trust you, they won't follow or respect you, and they will always wonder if you're being honest.

In previous chapters, I discussed how becoming a great manager means to stop worrying about your own career and to begin spending your days focusing on developing employees.

While working with College Summit in West Virginia, one of my younger employees, Jody Pauley, told me that he had been offered a job opportunity with a company that could provide him with financial stability to start a family. I had invested a lot of time with Jody, mentoring him and coaching him to become proficient at sales. I had originally hired him as my development assistant, watched as he moved up through the organization into another role. I believed that he was in line to do much greater things in the future for College Summit, possibly even becoming an executive and taking over my position in five to seven years. He was very talented and just a natural-born leader.

But I also knew that if I truly had Jody's best interests at heart, I had to encourage him to take advantage of this tremendous career opportunity with a well-established company. Although Jody left College Summit, he remains a friend. I frequently hear reports from professionals throughout West Virginia who tell me that Jody has become a *great* salesperson. Today, Jody is also minister of a church.

I recall another employee I mentored long ago at the large customer service center. One day, this young manager and I were talking. He asked me for feedback about his management skills and development. I said, "Sometimes you're a smart ass 22-year-old."

He looked at me with a somewhat confused look, but after a long pause, "Coming from anyone else, I would be angry, but coming from you, I know you just want me to be the best I can be. What can I do better?"

He was absolutely right; I wanted only the best for him.

This manager was one of the brightest young professionals I have *ever* mentored during my entire career. He had nearly unlimited potential, but I felt at times he wasn't taking the time to truly learn and appreciate all that I and others were trying to teach him. I shared this feedback with him – to help him improve and learn.

He was my best and most intelligent manager, so I only wanted him to thrive in this role – and in other roles later in his career. I felt that the best way to help him become a better manager on that particular day was to capture his attention by giving him that frank, unfiltered feedback, before going into more detail. He accepted the feedback for the gift it truly was, because I had invested sufficient time to build a very positive relationship with this young manager.

Now in his 40s, my former manager owns his own very successful business and remains a great friend. From time to time, we'll talk about the time I gave him the candid feedback and we'll both enjoy a good laugh.

I'm positive along the way he's taken a few young people under his wing – and I'm hopeful that he's given them the same gift of unfiltered, frank coaching to help them grow.

△ △ △

One of the most important keys to becoming a great manager is taking the time to develop relationships with employees you manage so that they know without a doubt that you are always looking out for their best interests. If employees you manage can't or won't trust you, they won't follow or respect you, and they will always wonder if you're being honest.

Several years ago, I worked with an organization whose top executive not only misled employees about the purpose of information she requested, but also regularly took personal credit for the work of her team, without sharing this recognition with her employees.

I recall learning from someone outside of the organization that this leader took credit for writing a successful proposal that produced over a half million dollars in revenues. The only problem was that I had worked nearly two weeks crafting the written proposal, while the executive had provided what amounted to only minor editing.

Don't misunderstand me. I wouldn't have minded even one bit *sharing* credit for this proposal as she played a role in editing it. If she had told someone that we *both* had written it, I wouldn't have been offended – not at all. I've always been more interested in getting the job done than getting credit. But to not give me *any* credit whatsoever when talking to someone outside of the organization? That was a bit much.

Once employees learned what this executive was doing to me and to others, the organization experienced an exodus of people – people who truly loved their jobs and were committed to the organization's work, but could not trust this leader.

Whenever you lead talented employees who love their jobs and are *completely* dedicated to the work, you should do everything possible to retain them, which of course includes being upfront and honest – and giving your employees recognition for their hard work.

I could never quite understand why this executive could never give her employees credit. From all indications, she felt threatened by her team's tremendous talents, instead of feeling great pride in knowing, "My team did this great work – and I was their leader!" She clearly did not have mindset of a coach.

I have also done some work for a couple of organizations whose top management badmouthed employees at every opportunity – behind their backs. At one organization, the top executive regularly had something negative to say about every single employee. As one would expect, neither of those organizations was truly successful. They may have had a few years of success, but lacked consistent, sustained growth, largely because they could never retain their best people.

Consistently, I have stood up for employees, recognizing their positive attributes, not just focusing on any shortcomings they might have had. To me, everyone has value.

Key executives at one organization absolutely *despised* one of my employees. They practically begged me to terminate her employment, but I refused. Although this employee struggled somewhat with one facet of her job, she thoroughly enjoyed performing another one of the major tasks that other employees didn't enjoy. This employee was also very conscientious and was just a really good person.

So what did I do? I minimized the amount of time she spent each day performing the task she wasn't proficient at doing, and maximized the time she spent doing what she was great at and thoroughly enjoyed. Doesn't that just make a lot of sense? Isn't that what a manager should do – make the best use of available talents and interests? Being a great manager isn't seeing how many people you can fire, but how you can best utilize talents at your disposal!

I also did some work with one organization whose top management talked terribly about every single person that left, whether they accepted another job or were terminated. It became a running joke among remaining employees that whoever left next would be blamed for *all* of the organization's problems during the previous six months – and for the entire next year!

The trust was completely broken by management, because employees knew without a doubt that they would be denigrated once they left.

△ △ △

Effective management looks at problems as opportunities to find solutions, not just to assign blame. Let me show you a better way of addressing mistakes.

While serving as Director of Communications for Kanawha County Schools, our department assembled information for and then printed a large directory with school contact information and addresses, as well as employees' names, their addresses and phone numbers, which was used for internal use only. As this was a system with nearly 100 schools and several hundred employees, the directory was well over 100 pages. I assigned the task of proofreading this directory to our department's secretary and desktop publisher.

Once the directory was printed, I and few others immediately noticed that a few lines of information were missing at the top of a single page in the directory. I called the two employees, Pat Hunter and Karen Taylor, into my office.

"What happened?" I asked.

"I thought Pat had checked that page, and she thought I had. We were busy with other projects, so we worked this into our schedules as we had time. We apparently both missed this one page," Karen explained.

"So, what can we do to ensure this won't happen again?" I questioned.

"What we will do from now on is put our initials on the proof for those pages as we check them. That way, we'll be able to tell for certain if the page has been checked and who checked it."

"Good idea," I said. "That's all. Thank you both."

"You're not going to yell at us?" Karen asked. "When we've made mistakes in the past, we've been yelled at."

"Why would I yell at you? This was an honest mistake," I explained. "You two are *great* employees. It's more important to determine how we can prevent this from occurring again than assigning blame. After all, ultimately it's my responsibility for ensuring work is done correctly and for making certain processes are in place to prevent mistakes."

The employees were absolutely amazed that I didn't yell at them for the mistake. Miscues will happen – even with the best, most talented employees. These two certainly fit in that category!

I've found over the years that terrible managers will spend a lot of time in "problem mode," focusing on the "blame game." "Problem mode" is when a manager focuses on the issue – who should be blamed and why the mistake occurred. Managers who focus on problems will sometimes belittle and berate employees for making mistakes.

Conversely, the best managers I have worked with during my career spent most of their time in "solution mode" when issues arose, developing processes to correct the root causes of mistakes so they would not happen again. Their viewpoint was that the mistake had already been made – so "Let's move on, fix it and figure out a way to ensure the same type of mistake never occurs again."

If a mistake occurs in your organization, which approach is more productive long-term – focusing on who did what and assigning blame, throwing others under the bus so you can look better – or trying to develop processes so the mistake won't happen again?

When I discussed the directory mistake at a Kanawha County Schools' management team meeting later that week, I took full responsibility for the mistake and didn't even mention how or why the mistake was made. I simply said we were implementing new procedures to ensure the mistake would not happen again.

Ultimately, the mistake was *my* fault because I did not ensure that processes were in place to prevent miscues from occurring – and I didn't proofread the directory.

△ △ △

At various times during my career, I noticed that a few employees would sometimes become angry or simply "shut down" when provided negative feedback from other managers. I believe this typically happens because the manager hasn't invested enough time developing a positive relationship with his or her employee.

With every positive comment about an employee's work or taking the time to ask sincerely about an employee's family, I envision the manager making a "deposit" into his or her relationship with that employee. From time to time, though, because of performance issues, a manager may need to make a "withdrawal" from that relationship in order to provide negative feedback. If the deposits add up to more than the withdrawals, the employee is less likely to become angry or to shut down and more likely to listen to the feedback because he or she knows all you're wanting to do as a manager is help him or her to learn and develop.

If you spend much more time "building up" your employees than "tearing them down," you will also create a culture of belief – belief that your organization and its employees have nearly unlimited potential and that you have your employees' backs.

I think the dynamic of employees "shutting down" is relatively easy to understand. Managers who invest sufficient time recognizing their employees for great work and getting to know their employees are communicating clearly that they are always looking out for their employees' best long-term interests – even when negative feedback is given. After all, the purpose of corrective feedback isn't to hurt an employee's feelings or to damage an employee's psyche; it's to help improve the performance of an employee and to make the organization more efficient and stronger.

Conversely, managers who do nothing but complain about employees or chastise them for a mistake or two will find that employees become angry, quit caring and eventually find other employment. I've seen this occur in a few corporations, in non-profits and for-profits, school systems, as well as in the smallest businesses.

At one organization, I and several other employees listened as one executive cursed at an employee so loudly that his yelling could be heard by everyone in the entire building. While working with another organization, I was told by an employee that he had witnessed a fellow employee being "talked to like a dog" by a manager – in front of both employees and non-employees.

Clearly, this is not effective management. People who treat others in this manner should *never* lead others. There is no excuse whatsoever for this behavior.

We successfully manage people *into* organizations through positive hiring and training experiences, but we also manage people *out* of organizations through consistently negative comments and micromanaging.

Unfortunately, when you manage large numbers of employees, you will also likely have to terminate the employment of a few, which is one of the most challenging and difficult tasks any manager will ever have to perform. In the case of every employee I made the decision to end his or her employment, I had to know that the termination was in the best interests of the employee and the organization. Even though the few employees I terminated may not have believed this at the time, their moving on to other opportunities was also in their best interests.

Before ever firing anyone, I first had to know in my heart that I had done everything possible to help the employee become successful. The only exceptions to this rule were when employees falsified records or clearly did not have the attitude or temperament to be successful (i.e., treating other employees, customers or clients terribly). In those cases, there was nothing I could do to transform a dishonest employee into an honest one – or an employee who clearly hated serving customers or clients into one who would.

Prior to ending the employment for anyone in recent years, I have also asked myself three key questions: 1) Does the employee make our organization better, or would we be better off without this employee? 2) Does the employee improve the quality of work for those working with him or her, or would other employees' work and even their quality of life be improved without this employee? 3) If I had it to do all over again, would I have hired this employee?

If, after asking myself these questions and realizing that the employee in question wasn't making our organization better, wasn't improving the quality of work or life for others and that I would never have hired this person if I had a "do over," I knew that my decision to end the employment for that person was the right one for the employee, the organization, its other employees and for me.

Looking back over my entire career, my only regrets were when managers or executives I reported to made personnel decisions *for me* or didn't allow me to take the appropriate steps that needed to be taken. Considering those few personnel issues now, I wonder if I should have been more forceful in my opposition.

I can now see that most of these decisions made by others were terrible ones for the organization – because those working above me had not invested enough time with employees to see what was *really* occurring. They did not know all that I knew, because they had not invested sufficient time learning about employees and their quality of work as well as their dedication to the job.

Sadly, this occurs in nearly every organization at one time or another – those in upper management with little first-hand knowledge making personnel decisions. I've seen it occur in organizations of all sizes – and it's a *huge* mistake.

Looking back on my career, I have no regrets whatsoever about standing up forcefully for what I believed in, but I do regret a couple of times that I possibly could have stood up more forcefully.

Peak Performance Chapter Activities:

1) Before terminating the employment of anyone, can you honestly say that you did everything you could to help your employee become successful?
2) What are your biggest personnel regrets?
3) What did you learn and how can you avoid these regrets in the future?
4) Are you quick to assign blame when members of your team are responsible for issues, but also quick to claim credit when operations are successful?
5) How do you treat or talk about employees who leave your organization?
6) What messages are you sending to existing employees with your comments and treatment of those who leave?
7) If an issue occurs, do you spend more time in "problem mode," or do you invest more time in "solution mode?"

Chapter 11: People and Numbers

As my construction worker father told me many years ago, "They can put anything on paper and people will believe it."

I have to admit that I've always been a "numbers guy." I love numbers. Numbers don't lie. But I have also learned during my career that numbers may not always tell a complete or accurate story – and that they provide data *after* the fact. This is one reason why you first must manage people – to understand what is occurring within your organization in real time and to determine if the data you're provided is accurate.

When I managed executives in Los Angeles, Miami, Indianapolis, West Virginia and Connecticut – all at the same time – I spent nearly an entire week every month with each of my teams in those locations. I tried to develop strong, positive relationships with my executives and their teams at each site so they would learn to trust me enough to tell me what they needed to do their jobs, and to share concerns as well as their successes. I coached, mentored and managed my employees all over the country with the sole purpose of helping them to become the best they could be.

Yes, I tracked performance through sales reports, but I already knew what the numbers would show me long before the reports were run.

As a result, there were no surprises.

I accompanied these executives on major sales meetings, sometimes chiming in a key point or two when they asked me to participate in the presentation. Typically, though, I would just sit back and watch them so I could later offer coaching, providing them with suggested, minor tweaks to their pitches or presentations.

The executives I led while with College Summit were some of the hardest-working, most dedicated and dynamic leaders I've ever had the privilege of working with during my career. Each came from a different background and brought a little different perspective, but each also had a level of commitment and talent that allowed him or her to excel.

I invested the time to ask employees about their families, hobbies and interests. I also took the time to show employees that I cared about them as people first and foremost. Since I spent so much time at each site developing relationships, my executives and their employees trusted that whatever advice I would provide was always in their best interests.

One of my most prized possessions is a signed football from my talented and very cohesive Indianapolis team, with all of the employees' signatures – J.T., Derrick, Shonda and Nicole – with the inscription:

Thanks for "blocking" for us.
- Team Indy

I did "block" for them quite a bit. I gladly did this for all of my teams across the country.

That's the difference between *quality management* and *micromanagement*. Quality management brings a "we're in this together" or "I'm here to help you" attitude, while micromanagement elicits an "I'm telling you what to do, how to do it and when to do it" type of arrogance. Quality management creates trust, respect and a positive relationship between manager and employees. Micromanagement creates a lack of trust and respect, as well as a strained, resentful relationship between manager and employee.

When you develop relationships with your employees, you also feel more comfortable having those difficult conversations when their performance may be slipping, because your employees know you are coming from a "good place." In addition, you're typically able to identify and correct *minor* issues before they become *major* ones.

Yes, numbers are vitally important when managing within any organization. Numbers can tell you if your organization is profitable, which departments are most profitable and which departments are adding little or nothing to the bottom line. Typically, these reports are backward-looking, though, informing you how your organization and departments *performed*.

Leaders who make management decisions based on these reports often struggle to make the correct decisions – or are late taking action – because they're making changes within their organizations based on data 30, 60 or even 90 days old.

I've done quite a bit of boating on major lakes. Imagine watching the wake of waves forming *behind* your vessel and deciding which direction to steer your boat as it moves *forward*. There could be a huge log in the water ahead that could sink your craft, but you would never see it, because you are looking *backward*. In essence, this is how you're managing if you rely solely or mostly on backward-looking data to lead your teams and to make needed corrections.

But if you invest the time necessary to develop positive relationships with your employees, you will know with great certainty what is going on within your organization, with its clients and customers – *in real time and even in the foreseeable future*.

You will also learn enough to question the numbers.

△ △ △

Let me show you how data, although accurate, may not always tell the full story.

While working with College Summit as Executive Director for the West Virginia office, we received college enrollment data for the schools we served. The data we received from our national office assessing our work were not impressive – not at all. Schools we served saw a very slight increase in their college enrollment rates, but those increases were about half what schools in other regions of the country were experiencing. Needless to say, our team was extremely disappointed in the data.

I knew from our work in schools that we were having a positive impact on college enrollment, but I also knew that the state had tightened the requirements a couple of times in previous years for its Promise Scholarship, which provided free tuition for eligible students throughout the state. I wondered, "Could these changes in available financial aid have had a negative impact on our results – and by how much?"

Not leaving this data analysis to anyone else, I began examining the numbers. I pulled college enrollment data for all 55 counties from the state website for each of the previous years, and then pulled out the data for the dozens of schools we were actually serving during that time frame to compare the performance of College Summit schools to the rest of the state. Essentially, I used non-College Summit schools as the control group. I compared the overall college enrollment rate of our schools in West Virginia to those in the state that weren't served by College Summit, creating two different sets of state college enrollment data.

The data showed me that while college enrollment rates had actually declined across the state because of much stricter requirements for the Promise Scholarship, the enrollment rates for the schools we served had actually increased, despite dramatic changes in available financial aid.

By plotting this data for the previous years on a PowerPoint graph, I was able to show a clear and ever-widening divergence in college enrollment rates for College Summit and non-College Summit schools. The college enrollment rates for the schools we served were clearly rising while data for the rest of the state were trending lower. In fact, because we were serving so many schools, the uptick in college enrollment in our schools helped to mitigate the true impact of the changes in the Promise Scholarship, making the state data look better than it really was. At the time I analyzed the data, we were serving about one-sixth of all seniors in West Virginia, which provided sufficient data across a large enough cross section of schools and districts to demonstrate the true statistical impact we were having on college enrollment.

Although this analysis required a couple weeks of number crunching, my data proved that we were having a *significant* impact on college enrollment in the schools we served in West Virginia! The data were very conclusive.

I shared this data analysis with executives at our national office. They were impressed with the results and with the West Virginia team's performance in improving college enrollment rates against what were clearly strong headwinds because of the major changes in available financial aid. We also shared this data with state higher education officials, who not only confirmed the data, but were quick to point out the clear and growing deviation in college enrollment data among College Summit and non-College Summit schools.

Several months later, I also shared this data with the State Superintendent of Schools, who commented that College Summit was one of the few educational programs in West Virginia with *proven* data to show that the program actually worked. Later, he requested a written proposal to implement College Summit across the entire state!

While most College Summit Executive Directors probably accepted the data from our national office at face value, I didn't. I knew enough from our work in schools all over West Virginia that I believed the data were not telling the whole story. After researching and analyzing the data, I was able to see *how*, but most importantly, *why*.

Later, I coached and mentored a College Summit executive, Alexis Shah, in Los Angeles when I served as Managing Director for Site Operations. While Alexis didn't fully understand data at first, she became a true data expert, partly because of my coaching but mostly because of her sincere interest in proving through numbers that what her team was doing was making a difference. This was one example of the student learning more than the teacher. Seeing Alexis learn about data and actually outpace my level of knowledge in this subject is one of the highlights of my career.

The best managers invest sufficient time with their employees to know results before data are available, but are also intelligent enough to question and analyze data themselves.

In short, the most effective managers are great "people persons," but they also understand and are able to analyze the data they are provided. Managers should be able to analyze data, but, sadly, a few can't or won't.

△ △ △

Having worked for and consulted with almost four dozen organizations in nearly every market sector during my career, I have seen it all in terms of data analysis – good, bad and terribly-flawed.

Several years ago, I was asked by a medium-sized company's executive management to analyze data for its sales team. I was provided a temporary log in for the sales data collection system and started dissecting the numbers. These executives knew that I had extensive management experience and apparently believed I could help their sales team and its manager become more effective.

At this company, as is the case with most businesses involved in sales, employees were provided names of interested, potential clients (leads) then were tracked and measured according to how many dollars they produced per qualified lead. Whether selling products such as copiers or services such technology consulting, nearly all organizations assess the effectiveness of their sales teams in a similar manner – how many dollars have been generated per qualified lead.

Within five minutes of examining the data, I noticed that the top-performing salesperson for this company in terms of dollars produced per lead was not providing a formal, written proposal to a large percentage of her potential clients. I also noticed that a large percentage of her leads were deemed to be unqualified – the client wasn't available at the assigned meeting time or requested products or services that the company did not provide. The amount of money this salesperson generated per lead was considerably higher than other members of the sales team, but I also noticed that the other sales people were consistently providing written proposals 20 to 30 percentage points higher than the top-performing salesperson. This was a huge red flag.

This salesperson may have been "playing with the numbers." Let me illustrate with simple dollar figures how easily this can be done and the true impact on any company's ability to collect accurate, meaningful data.

Let's say Salesperson A (Bill) and Salesperson B (Madge) is each provided 10 leads.

Bill only leaves proposals with seven of his potential customers. Although Bill travels to meet with all of the potential customers, he decides that three of the customers simply cannot afford his products or services and doesn't take the time to complete a proposal. Instead of leaving a written proposal, Bill simply marks the lead as "not available" or "wanted services not provided."

Conversely, Madge meets with all of her potential customers, and leaves a written proposal with each of the 10 potential customers, although she knows it's highly likely that three will never purchase services or products from her.

Bill closes three sales out of those leads, each for $5,000. According to the data in the company's system, he has sold three out of seven customers visited, which means that his conversion rate on qualified leads is 43 percent, with an average dollar per lead generated of $2,143 ($15,000/7). Madge makes three sales, too, each for $5,000. But since she submitted proposals to all 10 potential customers, her conversion rate is only 30 percent, and her average dollar per lead is only $1,500 ($15,000/10).

According to this company sales data, Bill is outperforming Madge by a wide margin – a conversion rate a full 13 percentage points higher and an average dollar per lead $643 or 43 percent higher. In reality, Bill and Madge are performing equally well, except Bill is only choosing to provide proposals for potential customers he knows have a much greater probability of buying – to make his numbers look better than they really are. This "playing with the numbers" happens frequently in companies of all sizes that quantify the performance of their sales teams and individual salespeople.

After analyzing the data, I approached the sales manager and asked him if he noticed that his top salesperson was providing proposals significantly less of the time than other salespeople on his team. The sales manager looked at the data and said, "I didn't know that."

That told me the sales manager clearly didn't understand or even look at his own team's data.

I did some further investigating and found that this sales manager spent very little time working with his people in the field, which meant that he had scant knowledge if data were accurate or not. In fact, I learned by asking a few key questions that he invested perhaps one day *per year* working with each salesperson in the field, although all of his salespeople were located in a relatively small geographic area.

This absolutely amazed me. When I managed sales teams in five cities from coast to coast at the same time, I invested three to four days in the field *every month* with each of my teams!

I wasn't surprised to learn that this manager's team was the worst performing division in the entire organization. This manager never invested the time to develop trust with his team, to coach and mentor team members, to understand each member's strengths and weaknesses so he *could* coach them, or even to determine if the data utilized to measure his team's performance was accurate and meaningful.

Realistically, every other department could have been performing exceptionally well and this company still would have struggled financially. An effective sales team is the revenue engine for every company, no matter how large or how small.

To use a basketball analogy, how can you effectively coach your team, if you haven't spent sufficient time watching your team play? How can you effectively lead your team if you don't pay attention to the score or if the results posted on the scoreboard are incorrect?

I reported back to executive management that they had *serious* issues with their sales team – first and foremost with the team's leadership.

△ △ △

Let me show you another example of the importance of doing work on the ground to learn the data – even *before* they become available.

While working as Director of Communications for Kanawha County Schools, I was asked to serve as the system's liaison for the school excess levy effort. One of the recent attempts at passing the levy had failed; previous attempts in recent years had passed by just a percentage point or two. In a large system such as Kanawha, the excess levy provided much-needed funds for maintenance and school programs.

We formed a small committee consisting of teachers union and service personnel representatives and a few students from schools, as well as a few interested key community leaders who supported the school system. The committee was officially led by a well-respected member of the community. On several Saturdays, our team walked door-to-door, asking voters in precincts overwhelmingly supportive of previous levies to support this levy, too. Our strategy was very simple: Do everything possible to encourage those who would support the levy to vote, while limiting communication to those who would most likely vote against the levy.

There was a good reason for our focused approach.

Several years prior, while attending a "Power in Politics," seminar with North Carolina Power/Virginia Power leadership, I learned that potential voters in every election should be placed in three categories, "Saints," "Sinners" and "Saviors."

The Saints are the voters you know will vote for you or for an issue – no matter what. The political expert who led this seminar said that this is the one group you want to focus the majority of your attention on – to encourage them to leave their homes and vote.

As for the Sinners, these are the people you know with very high probability will vote against you or against an issue. You want those people to stay home on Election Day, the expert said.

Saviors are the voters you might be able to turn around to your side, but you are never quite certain if you can. The political expert said that in any election you should focus very little of your attention on these voters, because you can never ever count on them – and they might actually turn out to be Sinners, voting against you or your issue.

In this levy election, we purposefully focused on the Saints – the regular voters we knew with very high probability would support the levy.

A few days before the election, during a Kanawha County Schools' management team meeting, I was asked if I believed the levy would be successful. Based on the feedback I had received from the team working to pass the levy, as well as my own first-hand observations while talking with potential voters, I provided an assessment.

"The levy will pass by an overwhelming margin, likely by as much as a two-to-one," I reported to the management team. "I actually believe it will pass by about 65-35."

A couple of the people on the management team actually started to laugh. Even the superintendent said, "If it passes by even a single vote, I'll be very happy."

The levy did pass. I believe the final tally, once all votes were counted, was 64-36 percent. I had a very clear idea what the data (election results) would show because I and others had invested sufficient time to talk with those who would be voting. Although no election is ever certain, I felt confident enough about our chances to make a prediction that was nearly right on.

My philosophy has always been to understand the "people" part of the equation first, before analyzing the data. Knowing the personnel side has always provided me with a much clearer view of what the data should show – and when to question the data.

As my construction worker dad told me many years ago, "They can put *anything* on paper and people will believe it."

What he was trying to tell me at an early age is that just because you may see or read something someone else prints or distributes, it doesn't mean the information is accurate or correct.

The most effective managers know when and how to question the data they're provided because they've invested sufficient time with their employees, clients and customers to know if it is accurate.

△ △ △

Let me share yet another example of the importance of data.

While leading marketing efforts for a small business a few years ago as Director of Business Development, I focused the company's advertising efforts and was able to improve our results dramatically. Instead of spending advertising dollars to promote products that very few customers would be interested in purchasing, I directed our advertising on products and services that would interest the largest number of potential customers. After all, television advertising is more like a shotgun than a rifle in terms of reaching potential customers. We also began using social media to advertise the company's products and services.

As a result of our efforts, we were able to spend significantly fewer dollars on television advertising (about 30 percent less), but were able to increase the number of customer inquiries (leads) from television advertising during the same time period (two years) by about 50 percent. Overall, we were also able to increase the total number of customer inquiries by about 70 percent over those same two years.

These results were possible because we focused our advertising efforts, and also because our call center and marketing teams meticulously tracked the sources of our leads – whether they were from television advertising, our website, social media, newspaper advertising, trade shows, radio advertising or even referrals from other customers. We also carefully assessed what our marketing cost by source.

I have to say that this small company had one of the most impressive marketing data collection systems I've seen for any business – large or small -- during my career.

Using this data, our marketing team focused efforts on those forms of advertising that provided us with the greatest number of customer inquiries at the lowest possible cost. As the company's Director of Business Development overseeing marketing efforts, I carefully watched this data daily, weekly, monthly and yearly. I compared results from one year to another so I would know if we were improving our marketing efforts over time. I knew *exactly* what was cost-effective with our marketing efforts – and what wasn't cost-effective. We knew down to the penny exactly how much every lead from each source ultimately cost our company.

Believe it or not, as this company was in the waterproofing business, we even tracked how well our marketing was performing in relationship to the amount of precipitation our service area received each and every month. Using the year before I started work as "baseline," we would track precipitation and leads each month to determine how well our marketing efforts were working and how much we were "over performing," based on historical data.

I actually believe this is very important data for companies whose businesses are weather-related. When I shared this data with representatives at the national headquarters for this dealer's network, managers there were astonished that we were able to track our efforts in such great detail. No one else in the entire network had apparently even attempted to determine the impact of weather on lead generation, although it seemed to be just plain old common sense to me and other leaders in this company.

I am utterly amazed at the number of managers I have worked with who have told me that they have no idea why their phones are ringing or why they're receiving inquiries from potential customers or clients. How can any business effectively manage its marketing and advertising budgets if management doesn't know what's effective and what's not? Without the data, you're only guessing – and may be wasting your limited marketing and advertising dollars!

As you have been shown throughout this chapter, data are vitally important for any organization – large and small. But the data must be tracked regularly and accurately – and managers must also know what the numbers show, after they first understand the "people" part of the equation.

Peak Performance Chapter Activities:

1) What data are most important in your organization?
2) Do these numbers tell you what is occurring now, what will occur in the future or what occurred in the past?
3) What information can you glean from your employees that will enable you to make organizational shifts based on real time data?
4) What information do you need from your employees to ensure your organization is nimble enough to make changes before market forces negatively impact your bottom line?
5) Do you receive data that you believe are flawed?
6) What can you do to ensure that your data provide you with meaningful, accurate information?
7) How can you analyze data in a more detailed manner to better understand that data – to ensure all of your numbers provide an accurate picture of your organization's performance?
8) Do you know for certain what marketing or advertising efforts are most effective for your organization?
9) If you answered "No," why not?

Chapter 12: Clear Vision

An organization's vision should be felt and truly believed by everyone working in that organization.

As a leader, you must have a clear vision of where you want to take your organization. In fact, everything you do as an organization must be done to propel you toward that vision, which is like the North Star for your organization and all employees. If an activity won't help your organization move closer to that vision, you clearly should not be doing it.

When I began working with Kanawha County Schools as Director of Communications, I established a clear vision of transforming our Communications Department into becoming a true public relations and communications arm of the school system, helping to spread positive news about all of the innovative programs and services the system was supporting to improve the education of young people. When I started work as Managing Director of Site Operations for College Summit, I had the vision of sharing what I had learned in West Virginia with teams all over America, helping to ensure more young people could transition to and be successful in college. And when I began work with North Carolina Power/Virginia Power as Director of Media and Community Relations, our team had the vision of transforming the utility from one hated by customers into one beloved by those same consumers.

At Kanawha County Schools, I began managing a Communications Department that was previously little more than a glorified print shop and secretarial pool. If I heard, "We've always done it this way" once after I started working there, I heard it a thousand times.

I really didn't care if the role of the Communications Department prior to my arrival was overseeing large copy jobs and providing secretarial support for other departments; that was not going to be our team's principal role now.

Our team started a monthly employee newsletter with articles about employees and innovative programs in our schools. We began producing a weekly television news show sharing information with cable viewers throughout the county – a show I hosted and produced. We wrote and distributed hundreds of press releases informing the public through the news media about all of the innovative programs being implemented in the system's schools. We also stopped using two of our department's employees as the secretarial pool for the school system, because we were doing different and much more important work – improving the perception of the school system in the many communities we served.

To achieve the goal of transforming the system's communications, I established a personal goal of visiting and generating positive publicity for every one of the system's nearly 100 schools. I achieved this goal, but it took over a year and a few thousand miles of travel from the central office to the various schools throughout the county.

I remember two comments in particular that reinforced I had made the right decision to establish this vision for our team and then strictly adhering to it. A parent I had never met called in one day out of the blue to talk with me.

"I have to say that communications from this system are the best they've ever been," the father explained. "If there's a bus accident, we know if our kids are safe. If there is a new program at the school, I read about it in the newspaper or learn about it on your television show. Thank you for improving communications in this system."

The second comment came from my very talented desktop publisher, Karen Taylor.

"I didn't think you could do it, but you did," she said. "You transformed us into a true communications department. I have seen more changes here in a couple of years than I had seen in my entire career!"

Actually, *we* transformed the department. I may have been the leader, but I had a very talented team that did the heavy lifting.

Randy D. Shillingburg

While working with College Summit as Managing Director of Site Operations, I traveled to a different city nearly every single week, training and coaching executives all over the country. We worked relentlessly, helping to transform the college-going culture in communities across America. My West Virginia "twang" may have been easily noticed by school system personnel in Los Angeles, Indianapolis, Miami or Connecticut, but my passion and our teams' commitment to helping students transition to education and training after high school stood out even more. I coached my executives to utilize college-enrollment data to prove that what they were doing was making a difference – and to tweak their programs to make them more successful.

I also shared what I had learned about building successful teams. Together, we tracked team growth with a detailed survey identifying all of the components of a highly-successful College Summit office. We assessed our progress building a strong, effective team, just as we closely followed sales, revenues and college enrollment rates. While other companies and organizations across the country were struggling to grow in a faltering economy, the College Summit teams I provided executive oversight for experienced consistently strong revenue growth.

I was fortunate to lead great people and wonderful teams who embraced this vision of changing the college-going culture in schools all over America – and were willing to work very hard to achieve this goal. I was their coach, mentor and strongest supporter.

At North Carolina Power/Virginia Power, I joined a division of Dominion Energy that was clearly failing. The year before I started with the company, it was known as Virginia Electric and Power Company, VEPCO, before a name change and rebranding effort. Service and rates were so terrible that the Governor of North Carolina had asked the company to sell its service area to another electric utility. When many local customers even said the name, "VEPCO," they would have this scowl on their faces, almost as if they had eaten a rotten piece of fish.

But our division management team had a vision. We became more involved in the community – philanthropically and through employee involvement. We started a corporate employee volunteer program that won an award from the President of the United States, and we initiated a Community Advisory Panel (CAP), one of the first such groups for any company in the entire country.

Under the leadership of Southern Division Vice President Jim Earwood and later Jim Frazier, our entire division and all of its employees began putting customer needs first. Even when we had power outages and our customers' lives were disrupted, communications were exceptional, regular and very empathetic. We would fax out at least four press releases every single day with updated restoration information whenever large numbers of customers were without power – and we would continually let customers know that we cared and were doing everything humanly possible to restore their electricity quickly.

Within five years, our division management team and employees transformed our division from having the *worst* customer perception results in the entire company to having the *best*. Customers would even tell us that they *hated* VEPCO, but they *loved* this new company.

The makeover was dramatic. In fact, when we asked for the largest rate increase in the mid-1990s (the largest rate increase to date in the company's history in North Carolina) the North Carolina Utilities Commission required us to hold five public hearings. At those five hearings, a *grand total* of three people showed up. Two attended just to tell the utilities commission what a great company we were, and the third voiced opposition to the rate increase, but also stated that we were a great, customer-focused company.

Successful organizations have a clear vision that everyone in the organization knows and completely understands. I have seen this same phenomenon in Fortune 500 companies all the way to small businesses, government agencies and even non-profit organizations. Those organizations in which the vision isn't crystal clear to everyone will struggle financially or operationally.

While many organizations spend several hours if not two or three days choosing just the right words for their "Vision Statement," these statements are typically nothing more than words, I have seen consistently seen. An organization's vision should be *felt* and truly *believed* by everyone working in that organization. Everything anyone in the organization does every single day should help it achieve that clear vision.

If there are seven words I would use to describe the organizations I've led, worked with and have done consulting work for that achieved greatness, those words would be: *Relentless in the pursuit of their vision.*

Over the years, I've also done some work with a few businesses that lacked a consistent focus. Perhaps because they struggled to make payroll and lacked effective leadership, a few small companies in particular continually searched for new, additional ways to grow revenues, instead of investing their time, limited dollars and management efforts perfecting what they did really well. By changing or shifting their focus, they were no longer relentless in the pursuit of a *singular* vision.

No organization can be good at everything, but every organization should be *great* at one thing. Those successful organizations –the largest Fortune 500 company, the smallest local business or a statewide non-profit – know this and focus their efforts on being the best in the world at what they do.

Peak Performance Chapter Activities:

1) What is your organization's vision (not Vision Statement)?
2) Would all employees in your organization be able to communicate that same vision?
3) If your answer is "no," why can't they?
4) If your answer is "no," what is your organization doing that is making its employees not believe or see that vision?
5) Are *you* relentless in the pursuit of your organization's vision?
6) Who on your team can be described as "Relentless in the pursuit of your organization's vision?"

Chapter 13: Learning from Others

Over the years, I have thought about what I learned from my four-year-old: A different point of view can often result in solutions that others simply can't see.

While playing the computer game, "Lemmings" some 25 years ago, I progressed to a level that appeared to be impossible to solve. I worked several hours over a two- or three-day period on this single level, attempting every possible combination of brick-laying, exploding and digging Lemmings to advance. No matter what combination I tried, I could not save a sufficient number of Lemmings to move on to the next level. It was *impossible* to move to the next level, I believed.

"Let me try this *lebel*, Dad," my four-year-old son, Morgan, said to me after seeing my frustration. (Yes, he said, "lebel.") Jokingly, I said, "OK, son," believing that allowing a child to work on a problem that had stumped an adult for several hours was a *complete* waste of time.

Imagine my surprise when he solved the puzzle in less than two minutes. By accidentally scrolling the screen view all the way to the right, he found an alternative exit that allowed him to easily save every single Lemming. Playing this game through dozens of levels over the previous two or three months, I had never seen an alternative puzzle on any level. I was constricted by my own set of rules and beliefs, while my young son wasn't.

Over the years, I have thought about what I learned from my four-year-old: A different point of view can often result in solutions that others simply can't see.

I regularly asked for feedback from my employees because I knew that those who were doing the work every single day would often have insight that could make our organization more efficient and financially stronger. At times, front-line employees won't be able to see the big picture and their ideas aren't always feasible, but more often than not their concepts can be implemented as is or with minor adjustments.

Having worked with so many different organizations as an employee and as a consultant, I have learned a lot from nearly every person I've worked with during the past 37 years. I have always been like a sponge, soaking up a little knowledge from every person who has touched my life and career.

Especially while with College Summit, I worked with dozens of talented, highly intelligent people, most of whom were 20 or even 25 years younger. It would have been easy to ignore their input – very stupidly and arrogantly thinking that I had so much more experience than they did – but I didn't. I wanted to learn from them, just as they wanted to learn from me. We discovered *together* as we were building and growing this organization.

While managing executives and their teams across the country for College Summit, I encouraged a collaborative decision-making process with even the youngest, least experienced employees having input into nearly every decision. In fact, I would lead each of my teams through a detailed survey every few months that actually assessed their progress toward building truly collaborative teams.

If you manage, you can glean a lot of helpful information about your organization from employees, but a few misguided managers believe they can never learn anything from the people who report to them. In organizations of all sizes and types, I've seen a few managers who would never take the time to listen – or to even ask their employees for input.

Time and time again, I have seen that this is a critical mistake that costs organizations of all sizes, short-term and long-term.

Peak Performance Chapter Activities:

1) On a scale of 1-10, with 1 being very low and 10 being the highest possible interaction, rate yourself on how effectively you listen to employees' ideas.
2) Ask your employees to rate you anonymously in the same way.
3) If there is a large disparity in the way you rate yourself and the way employees rate you, purposefully change your management style to incorporate more opportunities to encourage employee input – and then truly listen to that input.
4) What have you learned from each member of your team?

Chapter 14: Goal Setting

A more collaborative goal-setting and performance review process ensures greater employee buy-in, stronger communication and the ability for managers and executives to learn what is occurring within their organizations.

In the last few organizations I have worked with or provided management consulting services for, I have utilized or implemented a collaborative performance management system to establish goals for employees and to measure their performance.

I would meet with the employee to establish goals at the beginning of the new fiscal year. We would discuss both sales/revenue and customer service goals, as well as individual improvement goals. Typically we would establish no more than five goals, and each of the goals would not be easy to achieve. My feeling was that I would much rather have my employees establish a very ambitious goal and have them not quite achieve it than establish a less-than-lofty goal and have them reach it very easily.

A two-hour meeting was scheduled with each of my direct reports, as we would invest the time to discuss each goal thoroughly. Although I made it very clear that I retained decision rights for the goals, this process was truly a collaborative effort. In fact, I can't think of a single occasion when the employee and I disagreed on final goals. After goals were established, the employee and I would each sign the goal sheet.

At the end of each quarter, we would schedule another meeting to discuss progress toward the goals. In some cases, goals might be altered because of changes in the market or because the organization shifted direction slightly. If any changes were made to the goals, the employee and I would sign the goal sheet once more. Again, the goals discussion was very collaborative.

At the end of the year we would complete what many organizations would call a performance review, but because the employee and I had discussions throughout the year, there were no surprises. In fact, if there were surprises, I would view this as I was not doing my job as his or her manager. The employee knew how well he or she was doing working towards mutually-established goals, and the rating was very simple, as all goals could be measured.

This process ensured that:

- Goals were ambitious
- Goals were established by both manager and employee
- Employees "bought in" to the goals
- Goals were measureable
- Goals could be changed during the year
- There were no surprises

Earlier in my career, the typical practice was that managers established goals and presented them to employees – at the beginning of the new fiscal year. At the end of the year, employees met with managers once more to receive their annual review, a stress-filled meeting for both employees and managers.

The workforce has changed – so should the goal-setting and performance review process.

The previous process ensured that:

- Goals were always "reachable" and if they weren't, employees didn't have a say anyway
- Goals were established solely by the manager
- Employees rarely "bought in" to the goals
- Goals may have been measureable
- Goals could never be changed
- Since the performance review occurred only once at the end of the year, there may be a few surprises at the performance review

A collaborative goal-setting and performance review process ensures greater employee buy-in, stronger communication and the ability for managers and executives to learn what is occurring within their organizations.

△ △ △

While doing some work with a company several years ago, I implemented this collaborative goal-setting process that included measurable goals and regular check-ins with employees to discuss their progress toward goals. The system I implemented replaced what was in place previously – no regular check-ins and vague goals that were the same for every employee and certainly could not be measured. The previous goals essentially were little more than "Do a good job."

How can goals such as these ever be measured? How will employees even know if they're doing their jobs well?

Despite my urging, the organization never tied its employee compensation, including performance bonuses, to the review process or even to the overall financial performance of the company. Instead, an arbitrary decision was made every year by the same executive about raises and bonuses.

I strongly advocated for more financial transparency and a more objective process to determine bonuses and raises so employees could better understand their contributions to the organization.

Just as goal-setting should be a collaborative and transparent process, I also believe employees' financial rewards should be more transparent and less arbitrary in most organizations.

My strong belief is that if you want your employees to feel true ownership and recognize the vital roles they perform, you will allow them to see more of the numbers and provide them with the ability to measure and even track their progress toward goals, as well as your organization's performance toward financial goals.

By making this process more *objective* (based on numbers and performance toward goals) and less *subjective* (personal attitudes and feelings), managers can easily explain decisions about raises and bonuses – and for employees to understand those decisions.

Peak Performance Chapter Activities:

1) Is your organization's goal-setting process collaborative and does it create true discussion among employees and managers – or is it more of a "manager talking to the employee" process?
2) Is your performance review process stressful for managers and employees?
3) Is your goal-setting process flexible, which means goals can be changed if market conditions or focus areas need to change?
4) How can you incorporate components of the goal setting process described in this chapter into your organization's performance management system?
5) How can you make your organization's decisions about raises and bonuses more objective and less subjective?

Randy D. Shillingburg

Chapter 15: More Winning

This company does its work every single day the way a growing company should operate – committed to treating employees and customers very well and "doing the right thing" with every interaction.

In addition to working for a large number of organizations, I have had the privilege of doing consulting work for organizations of all sizes and types – from the smallest businesses to large electric utilities and even worldwide chemical companies.

Within 10 minutes of entering any office, I can typically determine if that organization is successful, or if it's struggling to survive.

Advanced Heating & Cooling, a Morgantown-based HVAC company, is one of my favorite companies – ever. I remember a conversation I had a couple of years ago with Dave Seman, the President of this great small business, when I started providing his company with consulting services.

He told me that his company is successful *because* of his employees. Dave told me in no uncertain terms that employees "make me look good." Whenever I'm at his offices, I see the same very happy, very engaged employees each and every time – because there's very little turnover.

Employees are always smiling, totally dedicated to doing their jobs well, and more importantly, committed to providing their customers with exemplary service. I see this and *feel* this every day I'm working at Advanced Heating & Cooling's offices.

I hear employees' interactions with customers and see how often this company does everything possible to treat customers very well. Advanced Heating & Cooling is always searching for new, innovative ways to serve its customers more efficiently. Dave sends a strong message to his employees about how much he trusts them to always provide exemplary service. Instead of searching for excuses why they can't meet customer needs, as I have seen with a few businesses, large and small, Advanced Heating & Cooling consistently finds a way to go the extra mile and more for its valued customers. Dave only hires employees who share in this same strong commitment to quality service.

Advanced Heating & Cooling is a rapidly-growing company, but it is clearly committed to maintaining a family-like atmosphere and an unwavering commitment to customer service as it grows.

What I see from Dave and the entire leadership team at Advanced Heating & Cooling are the attributes I have seen in all "winning" managers:

- An unwavering belief in the team and its ability to succeed
- An unwavering positive outlook
- The ability to communicate the complex by making it simple
- The ability to set high expectations and then communicate those expectations *clearly* to team members
- The ability to inspire

The online reviews for this small company speak volumes about its employees and top-notch management. Customers routinely post comments about the company's unequaled professionalism, quick response time, great integrity and consummate customer service. This company completes its work every single day the way a growing company should – committed to treating employees and customers very well and "doing the right thing" with *every* interaction.

△ △ △

Conversely, I've done work with a few organizations that are the polar opposite of Advanced Heating & Cooling in terms of management attitudes and even financial performance.

Over the past three decades-plus, I've worked with just a few organizations whose top management blamed employees for all of their problems; companies that experienced extreme turnover every year; organizations that seemingly tried their best to avoid meeting customers' needs when there were issues; management that routinely belittled and even berated employees; and organizations that barely made or even missed payroll.

Consistently, these organizations struggled financially, when they should have been dominating their markets.

What I consistently saw with these few always-struggling organizations were the attributes of unsuccessful, ineffective management:

- A lack of belief and trust in team members
- A negative outlook (always looking for fault)
- The ability to make the simple very complex
- The ability to set low expectations or a failure to communicate expectations clearly
- The ability to instill fear and distrust among team members

I have consistently seen that management – not employees – is the only constant in organizations that consistently struggle. I've seen this in a few organizations of all sizes and in all market sectors.

Top management in these organizations can never see who to blame for their failures, because they can't seem to develop the self-awareness to look in the mirror.

Peak Performance Chapter Activities:

1) What is your organization's employee turnover rate?
2) Is your organization struggling financially?
3) After considering the first two questions, are you a "winning" manager or executive, or is your team struggling because of your leadership style or the leadership styles of your managers?
4) Is your company more like Advanced Heating & Cooling, or the examples of organizations that are always struggling?

Chapter 16: Inclusion

The worst decisions I have seen other managers and executives make were when they didn't provide the opportunity for employees to provide valuable input.

One of the toughest parts of being a manager or executive is realizing that, ultimately, the responsibility rests on *your* shoulders. At times, it's a very heavy burden and often creates significant stress.

But it doesn't have to be that way – and it shouldn't be. Your team will share the weighty load of driving your organization forward, if only you will ask your employees to help – and give them the *gift* of allowing them to help.

I'll explain more about my thoughts of this being a "gift," at the end of this chapter. I will provide you with a *completely different way* of looking at why you need to involve your employees more in the day-to-day operations and decision-making for your organization.

What I've seen during my career is that too few managers truly understand the importance of including their employees in the decision-making process and the responsibility for growing their organizations.

Today, "inclusion" is a common management catchword that means ensuring that all employees are treated fairly and respectfully, have equal access to opportunities and can contribute to the organization. While a workforce may be "diverse" in terms of skin color, religion, age, socio-economic and educational backgrounds, it may not always be inclusive. I believe that an organization cannot be truly diverse if it isn't also inclusive -- and that it cannot be inclusive if it isn't also diverse.

Unfortunately, in most organizations, inclusion seldom means actually *listening* to employees, their thoughts and ideas, or even providing them with the opportunity to lead. Taking the time to listen to employees doesn't negatively impact the decision-making process. It makes it much stronger!

To be an effective manager, you not only need to learn how to listen to employees, but you should also be willing to ask them to lead or facilitate the discussion. That means you, as a manager, have to surrender some power. For many, that's very intimidating and even scary.

While leading the College Summit West Virginia team, I facilitated very few team meetings during my last year as Executive Director. Although I maintained rights for a few major decisions, I trusted my employees to make the best decisions for our organization more often than not.

Instead of criticizing an idea in a team meeting that might result in employees feeling intimidated, I tried to ask leading questions to help them arrive at what I believed was the best decision for the organization. By asking a few questions, I was able to help all team members better understand the reasons for the decision our team made. In addition, I often learned valuable information that changed my mind to what other team members believed was the correct decision.

To me, decision-making was never about power, it was always about making the best choices for our team. Over the last quarter of my career, I began to see myself as more of a *facilitator* that steered and encouraged team members to determine the best decisions than a manager who *told* employees what to do.

When my College Summit employees in West Virginia were leading a meeting, the only role I typically played as their local executive was ensuring that all employees were heard. If I thought that one or two people were dominating a conversation, I might ask for input from the other employees, because they might have different and often vital information about the issue we were discussing. By asking questions, I tried to show employees how to determine the best direction for our team, instead of telling them what that direction might be. I was also "modeling" how I wanted my managers to lead their teams.

Which method do you think results in employees better understanding decisions and "owning" them, telling employees what to do or asking them leading questions to facilitate open, honest discussion?

The worst decisions I have seen other managers and executives make were when they didn't provide the opportunity for employees to provide valuable input.

During the last half of my career, I've had the opportunity to do quite a bit more facilitation – facilitating team meetings, executive team meetings for organizations, and even meetings among executives and managers for some of the largest corporations in America and key members of their communities. I've learned that facilitation is probably a manager's most useful tool, because it takes him or her away from the attitude of *leading* and *making decisions* to the mindset of *encouraging collaboration* and *quality decision-making* that bring about positive results.

The best managers understand this and bring people together. The least-effective managers never quite understand the importance of quality facilitation and shared decision-making.

△ △ △

Several years ago, while working with the West Virginia Department of Education, I developed a great friendship with a fellow manager who also worked in state government, but in another area. He talked with me extensively over several lunch meetings about what I would consider to be one of the worst examples of management – ever.

My friend told me that an executive (two levels above my friend) had made the decision a few months earlier to move some of the work my friend's employees were performing to another area in the same department of state government, but under another manager. As my friend explained, this executive made the decision without first discussing this idea with the manager in charge (my friend), without talking to any of the employees to learn more about the complex processes required to complete the work, and without even fully comprehending the scope of the work or the various regulations driving the operations. My friend explained to me that even the senior manager who reported directly to this executive (and supervised my friend) was *completely blindsided* by the executive's decision.

On top of this ill-informed judgment, this executive's intimidating and even threatening management style resulted in managers working under him being afraid to discuss the vital issues that needed to be resolved in order to ensure the successful transition of this work.

Based on what you've learned so far, do you believe this decision was a success or a failure?

I talked with my friend several months after the work had been moved to under the other manager. He said that the transition of work was a complete mess. Not only did more personnel than was originally anticipated have to be transferred in order to get the work done, but the exact same work was now requiring more than twice as much time to be completed.

In other words, this executive's decision ultimately required more employees to do the exact same work and it took more than twice as much time to get the same work done. That's definitely *not* progress!

I know that the office where this manager worked (he recently retired) is diverse in terms of skin color, religious beliefs, educational levels, socio-economic backgrounds and even age as mandated by state and federal laws.

But is this style of management encouraging diversity and inclusion, or is it simply checking off boxes in a government-required hiring process, completely ignoring the inclusion part of the equation? How can any organization be truly diverse if it isn't also inclusive? What is the purpose of having a diverse workforce if only a single voice is making decisions?

During my extensive career, I've experienced only a couple examples of intimidating, non-inclusive leadership, but, thankfully, nothing to the extent my good friend saw first-hand.

Working with and doing consulting work for several dozen organizations over the past three decades-plus, I have had the opportunity to see the decision-making processes for most of them up close. Fortunately, I have seen only two or three executives and managers who were strongly autocratic. For these few managers, whatever *they* decided was the edict throughout their "kingdoms."

Thankfully, I have worked with an exponentially larger number of executives and managers across the country who have utilized a more collaborative decision-making process, one that ensured more or even all voices were heard before any decision was made.

△ △ △

One of the most important lessons I've learned about management across all market sectors is that the quality of the process an organization uses to make a decision ultimately determines whether or not the results of that decision will be positive or negative. If the process is faulty because of incomplete information or a lack of feedback, then it is very likely that the decision itself will be flawed, too. However, if the process is detailed and includes viewpoints from everyone who might be affected, then the decision will most likely result in very positive outcomes.

What I've seen time and time again with organizations of all sizes is that there is a clear, *indisputable* correlation between the *quality* of the process used to make a decision and the *outcome* of that decision –whether it's a success or a complete failure.

I heard a joke several years ago that illustrates this perfectly.

A manufacturing company had a regular delivery scheduled to its facility every month. After changing delivery companies, the new truck driver maneuvers his semi-truck into the facility one day, only to discover that the large vehicle doesn't have sufficient clearance to drive under an overpass leading to the facility. The truck gets stuck halfway under the overpass.

Two mid-level managers in charge of shipping and receiving put their heads together and decide what to do. Their solution is to rent a crane to lift the overpass off of its supports once the bolts are removed, allowing the overpass to be raised high enough for the truck to pass. After the truck makes its delivery, the crane places the overpass back in place, and workers secure the overpass with large bolts.

The next month, another driver for the same company attempts to make the delivery. Once more, the truck becomes stuck. But this time, the managers know exactly what to do, so they rent a crane, have their employees use it to raise the overpass high enough so the truck can pass, and then have those same workers put the overpass back into place once the truck leaves the facility.

On the same day every month for several months, the delivery truck becomes stuck under the overpass. Each month the same mid-level managers decide that the best course of action is to rent a crane.

After seeing numerous invoices for crane rentals – and not knowing the reason for the rental costs – the company's Chief Financial Officer (CFO) does a cost-benefit analysis. He believes that it is utterly ridiculous for the company to be renting a crane each and every month!

Now for the punch line . . .

So, the CFO decides that in the long run, it would be much more cost-effective for the company to buy a crane and submits a request to executives for the purchase. Company executives, not knowing the reason for the crane rentals but seeing the detailed and very professional cost-benefit analysis provided by the CFO, approve the major capital expenditure.

A reasonable person, knowing the reason for the rental costs, would have communicated with managers of the delivery company, instructing them to bring a truck that wouldn't require as much vertical clearance. Or the company would have placed large signage before the overpass about the available clearance. Even letting a little of the air out of the tires might have allowed the truck to pass easily. Why not raise the overpass a few inches *permanently*, so trucks of that height could easily pass? There are so many potential solutions – all of which are a lot less costly than *buying* a crane. The lack of communication and quality decision-making in this organization resulted in a very costly, completely ridiculous capital outlay.

I enjoy this story and have told it many times because it is authentic to those of us who have worked with a variety of organizations. We've all seen managers who have made terrible decisions because of a lack of communication or a flawed decision-making process that didn't consider all relevant information before moving forward.

△ △ △

Allow me to share another real-world example of making decisions, transitioning work and implementing changes before all areas of the organization are prepared.

While working with North Carolina Power/Virginia Power in late 1993, I learned that executive management in Richmond had decided to centralize call center functions that were currently being performed in each of the company's division and district offices. On paper, this was a great idea and could potentially save the company millions, while providing better, more efficient service to customers. In fact, most major companies today centralize call center functions to save money and improve efficiency. Unfortunately, the company implemented this change too quickly, without fully understanding all of the ramifications of this change, and apparently without providing adequate training for those who would be taking the calls.

During an emergency situation on January 19, 1994, I was heard "live" on nearly every radio and television station in Virginia and North Carolina, urging customers to turn off non-essential appliances and also to explain the need for short rotating blackouts because of an emergency situation I will detail further in a subsequent chapter.

I received a call from the President of a Chamber of Commerce in North Carolina late that afternoon, who explained she had tried calling our company's new centralized call center. She told me her conversation with a customer service rep at one of the new centers in Virginia went something like this:

"I'm calling about the rotating blackouts for North Carolina Power," the Chamber President said.

"Ma'am, you're calling Virginia Power," the customer service rep replied.

"It's the same company," the Chamber President said. "I heard Randy Shillingburg on the radio earlier today talking about the rotating blackouts."

"We don't have rotating blackouts, ma'am," the representative answered. "We're Virginia Power, not North Carolina Power."

By now, the Chamber President was starting to get a little angry.

"Ma'am, I am *telling* you that your customers *are* experiencing rotating blackouts and that Virginia Power and North Carolina Power is the same company! I know because I work with this company's managers all of the time!"

In a rush to have this call center operational, someone in management apparently failed to properly train employees and, also likely forgot to ensure that important details of any emergency situation would be communicated quickly to the people who would be taking calls from customers. The representative at the Virginia call center didn't even realize that the company served customers in North Carolina – or that the company was cutting off power to groups of customers for a short time in Virginia and North Carolina in order to protect a fragile power grid because of an extremely cold day.

I calmly talked the Chamber President "off the ledge," so to speak, when she called me that afternoon. Yes, she was enraged when she first called, but she appreciated my taking the time to talk with her, even though it was one of my most hectic days ever with that electric utility. Providing this key community leader with personalized, friendly attention allayed her fears and anger – and helped to restore her faith in what was (and still is) a great company.

△ △ △

Mistakes can and will occur, even with the top-performing organizations. All it takes, though, is one manager not thinking through a situation, not gathering sufficient input from employees actually doing the work, not communicating well or not training employees thoroughly to damage the reputation of even the most customer-focused organization.

Sadly, I've seen this occur several times in government agencies, Fortune 500 companies, small businesses and even non-profit organizations during my career.

What I believe is that if you don't include affected employees and managers in the decision-making process, you're sending the clear message that:

- I don't value your input
- I don't trust your judgment
- I know best
- You know little

But when you include affected employees and managers in a collaborative decision-making process, you are also sending the unambiguous message that:

MANAGING TO PEAK PERFORMANCE

- I value your input
- I trust your judgment
- Together we will determine what is best
- You know a lot and I want to learn from you

Which set of messages do you want to communicate to *your* employees as you manage them – the first set or the second set?

You *will* include your employees in the decision-making process – if you want employee buy-in for these decisions and your desire is to determine the best choices possible for your organization.

△ △ △

Now to my final point – about how having employees help you is a wonderful and very gratifying gift *to them.*

I believe there's actually something much deeper occurring within humans when we resist sharing power with others or asking others for their help. Innately, I believe, many resist asking others for help because they believe it makes them appear to be weak.

Early on in my career with North Carolina Power/Virginia Power, I was talking with a friend and fellow manager, Billy Joe Wooten, who gave me some sage advice I have always remembered.

"Randy, you rarely allow others to help you," he said. "Don't you realize that one of the greatest gifts you can ever give to anyone else is the feeling of helping you? Why would you deny any friend of yours the opportunity to *receive* that gift?"

I realized when he said this that he was absolutely right, although I had never considered the impact of someone helping me in that particular way. As Billy Joe explained, the satisfaction of doing something for someone else is one of the best feelings any of us will ever experience as human beings – and the greatest gift we will ever *receive.*

Randy D. Shillingburg

In fact, study after study has shown that the happiest people on this Earth are those who regularly give to and do for others. Think about it – wouldn't this concept also apply to your employees as they do for you?

△ △ △

Several years ago, while living near Charleston, West Virginia, my next door neighbor was recovering from surgery and unable to mow his lawn. At the time, I was traveling for my job and was typically on the road from Monday through Thursday every single week.

Although he never asked me for my help, I used my riding and push mowers to trim his two-acre yard every week, sometimes twice a week – once on Thursday when I got home and occasionally a second time on Sunday to keep the grass from growing too high before I would be able to mow it again. I mowed his yard for nearly three months while he recovered. At the end of the summer, after he had received clearance from his doctor to resume normal activity, my neighbor walked over to my home to thank me, with tears flowing down his cheeks.

"Randy, this was probably the nicest thing anyone has *ever* done for me."

Seeing the look on this friend's face and knowing that I had helped another human being during his time of need was the most powerful, most meaningful gift I have ever *received* in my entire lifetime.

What I did for my neighbor wasn't the gift; what I felt by helping him at a time when he needed assistance was the true reward. To this day, I have this warm feeling in my heart and tears welling up in my eyes whenever I reflect how much my friend and neighbor appreciated my help. He gave *me* a wonderful gift!

Billy Joe was absolutely right. The advice he gave me not only applies to friends and family members, but also to the people who work with us.

My advice is to provide your employees with the same wonderful, uplifting gift of helping you and supporting you every single day. Include your employees in decision-making and allow them to be a valued part of *your* team.

Provide your employees with the greatest gift of all – allowing them to have the gratifying feeling of helping you and your organization succeed while playing an integral role in building something great.

Peak Performance Chapter Activities:

1) Is your workforce diverse? If not, why not?
2) How often do you allow your employees to lead meetings and discussions?
3) Do you make a lot of statements during meetings, or do you ask more leading questions to improve understanding and the quality of the decision-making process?
4) How do you ensure that all employees are heard during meetings?
5) How can you make your organization more inclusive in its decision-making process and not just diverse in its hiring process?
6) How can you give your employees the most meaningful gift ever – the gift of helping and supporting you?
7) What is your organization's process for making decisions? Does it ensure success by encouraging a collaborative process or does it ensure failure by limiting input from those affected?

Chapter 17: Onboarding

A lack of quality onboarding is nothing more than setting up new employees to fail.

As an organization grows, it becomes increasingly difficult to maintain the same culture and attitude of the original group of people who built it from the ground up.

To ensure that organizations maintain the same original culture, it's vitally important that they invest in "onboarding" new employees – helping them to acclimate and assimilate into the organization successfully.

While serving as Managing Director of Site Operations for College Summit, I helped to develop an onboarding process and then trained executives all over the country to acclimate themselves into our fast-growing organization.

Sadly, most organizations invest more time determining which copiers to purchase or lease for their offices than in developing a detailed onboarding process so that new employees can be brought on board successfully.

Based on my experience onboarding executives and managers in three organizations, I believe there are four key areas of onboarding necessary for any organization: Organizational Onboarding, Job-Specific Onboarding, Manager-Specific Onboarding and Relationship Transition Onboarding.

Let me explain each area.

Organizational Onboarding is the training required for an employee to be successful within a particular organization, no matter what role he or she might play. Organizational Onboarding should be a requirement for every new employee to ensure that he or she understands the culture, fully comprehends the requirements (i.e., time-reporting requirements, expense reports, company policies, parking, etc.) and expectations of being an employee within that organization, as well as helping the employee to understand the organization's history, Mission, Vision and Values.

In addition to meeting with the organization's founder or CEO to learn more about the established culture, the employee will also need to complete all necessary paperwork to become a new member of the team. If an organization is fully committed to bringing on new employees effectively and to help them become acclimated to the organization's culture, this Organizational Onboarding will be almost exactly the same for every new employee. The various facets of Organizational Onboarding will be spread throughout an organization, but will require a human resources professional or the employee's manager to schedule the needed appointments.

The second area of onboarding, **Job-Specific Onboarding**, is the training necessary for an employee to be successful in a specific role. Even the most experienced new employees will require training to perform their jobs, even if only to learn how a particular organization performs certain tasks within those roles. Typically, a manager or lead employee will perform this area of onboarding.

Manager-Specific Onboarding is the communication and collaboration between manager and employee, establishing job expectations and goals, and determining how they can work most effectively together. Whenever I onboarded a new executive, I always met with him or her near the end of the onboarding process to ensure Manager-Specific Onboarding was thoroughly covered. I wanted all new employees to understand my expectations, as well as their goals, so that they could become productive as quickly as possible. I also wanted to learn more about their expectations for me as their manager. The manager takes the lead in this area of onboarding.

The last area of onboarding, **Relationship Transition Onboarding**, is overlooked within many organizations. This is simply the introduction of the employee to the key contacts inside and outside the organization. In order to be successful, the new employee must understand who his or her internal contacts will be for nearly every issue, and may also need to meet external contacts who were already established by the previous employee in that role. In some cases, the employee being promoted or replaced may be asked to lead this area of onboarding, while in other cases the manager may need to initiate these introductory meetings.

Each area of onboarding is vital not only to the organization's success, but also to the new employee's ability to thrive within that organization.

Consider for a moment a company that ensures all new employees are provided Organizational and Job-Specific Onboarding, but aren't provided Manager-Specific or Relationship Transition Onboarding. The new employees will understand company policies and culture, as well as how to do their jobs, but may not fully understand what their manager expects and won't be introduced to vital internal and external contacts. New employees will understand their roles, but they may fail miserably in meeting their managers' expectations or in working collaboratively with people inside and outside the organization.

Yes, all four areas of onboarding are vitally important!

As I have worked across the country with a number of organizations, I have discovered that very few organizations, large or small, invest sufficient time and effort onboarding new employees, which is the principal reason why so many organizations begin to falter as they grow.

Most organizations never even invest the time to help new employees understand the corporate culture, its history or even to establish goals in the first couple of weeks employees are on the job. For many organizations, onboarding consists of "completing new employee paperwork" and showing the new employee his or her office or desk. Employees are then expected to learn with little or no assistance.

This lack of quality, detailed onboarding will result in either employees making mistakes, becoming frustrated and quitting, or learning on their own and, hopefully, surviving and then thriving within the organization.

A lack of quality onboarding is nothing more than setting up new employees for failure. I have seen that the top-performing organizations – and ones that are able to scale successfully – ensure that all of their new employees are acclimated to the culture and are provided sufficient guidance and training to be successful in their new positions.

Onboarding should never be viewed as "just another task" you have to complete among all of your other duties as a manager. This component should be prioritized as the first, most important step in helping your organization achieve peak performance as it grows.

Peak Performance Chapter Activities:

1) What is your organization's onboarding process?
2) On a scale of 1-10 with 1 being not effective at all and 10 being highly effective, rate your organization's process.
3) Which of the four areas of onboarding do you believe are adequately addressed with new employees?
4) Ask a newer employee what was missed or could be improved with your organization's onboarding process.
5) Which areas need further attention to ensure new employees are provided every opportunity to be successful?

Chapter 18: Process

Instead of telling my executives how to do their jobs, I helped to facilitate their developing processes for how they were going to achieve greatness with their teams.

The detailed process I developed to help new executives become acclimated to College Summit is just one example of the comprehensive manner in which I trained, managed and coached employees.

When I managed executives for College Summit all over the country, I focused on what I called the five P's: People, Prospecting, Pitch, Proposal and Product. Each of these five areas entailed a thorough process.

The "People" part of the equation was ensuring quality employees were hired who would fit well in the culture of the organization, establishing clear expectations for them, and then coaching/managing new employees to achieve the greatest possible success. Every step of the hiring and onboarding processes was strictly followed for every new employee, no matter where he or she was hired.

As for "Prospecting," this, too, was a process – the process we utilized to determine which potential customers and funders would provide us with the greatest opportunity for success. As I managed executives in the Prospecting process, we discussed and detailed how much time they would invest with existing customers, potential new customers and flywheel customers, ensuring there would be a balance to ensure steady, progressive growth in school sales. We also discussed how they could identify customers most likely to purchase our products and services.

The "Pitch" component was the time we actually invested developing and perfecting sales pitches to potential customers, from a one-minute "elevator" pitch all the way to a formal 20- or 30-minute presentation. As I attended many major sales presentations with my teams, I would provide employees with feedback after the meeting so that minor corrections could be made immediately, instead of wondering why sales were faltering months down the line.

We even mapped the processes involved with the "Proposal" part of the puzzle – ensuring we captured compelling testimonials and key information for proposals, determining how proposals would look and even what additional information we would collect to help our grant writers craft successful proposals.

As for our "Product," we discussed and outlined how often and when our teams would meet with school and community partners, ensuring that we provided consistent, quality contact to all partners throughout the entire year. The executives and I would also discuss the data we would share, how and when we would share this information – and even the various methods we would utilize to communicate our successes with partners.

As I provided executive oversight across the country, I emphasized all of these five critical components required to help them lead very successful teams. I helped *them* to develop nuanced approaches in order to accommodate community or cultural differences. As I worked with executives across the country in perfecting these processes, I would learn what their strengths might be, as well as the areas for which they might need additional assistance and support. This keen insight helped me to become a more effective manager and mentor for them.

While some may view this style of management as micromanaging, it really wasn't. I was willing to invest the time and effort to *help* my executives be successful.

We left nothing to chance. Instead of telling my executives how to do their jobs, I helped to facilitate *their* developing processes for how *they* were going to achieve greatness with their teams. My employees knew that I was working *beside them* every step of the way, doing everything possible to help *them* be successful. I wasn't an executive *telling* them how to get their work accomplished. I was viewed as a trusted team member who visited three or four days every month, providing sage advice and assistance at key points to help them become more successful and proficient at their jobs.

I was invested in *their* success, but I didn't do the work for them.

I facilitated the development of *processes* to ensure they would be successful. And by spending time with each of my teams every month, I was also able to quickly share innovations developed by one team with other teams across the country. That's yet another reason why the teams I managed performed so well. If I learned about an innovation developed by my Miami team one week, I would share it with my team in New Haven, Connecticut, the very next week when I traveled there.

In essence, I was a *traveling executive coach* who helped to ensure my teams across the country were well versed on the fundamentals of People, Prospecting, Pitch, Proposals and Product – just as I trained my elementary team decades ago on the fundamentals of basketball.

△ △ △

Compare the effort I invested to support my teams to the amount of effort and time expended by the sales manager described in Chapter 10, who clearly did not even understand his own team's data. At one point, I asked a member of his team what training he had received to learn a complicated new product line. He said he was tossed a thick manual by the sales manager – and was told to read it and understand it. *That* was the training, and he was expected to read it, comprehend it, and then go out and sell the very complex line of products!

This sales manager made no investment whatsoever in his team or in any of his sales people. How can you ever expect your employees to listen to or even respect you, if you don't invest sufficient time helping them to be successful?

△ △ △

Let me share two specific examples of processes I utilized at College Summit that helped me to lead my teams to improved performance and better communications.

While with College Summit, other managers and I began using two tools to help us manage more effectively, which I then passed on to all of my teams and encouraged them to utilize, too. One was a "How We Work Together" document or HWWT and the other was "What Was Said," or WWS.

The HWWT was a document that each of my teams produced to communicate simply and clearly how employees should work together. Through a process I first facilitated, each of my teams produced a document that detailed how employees would work and collaborate with one another. The purpose wasn't to produce a well-written, creative document; the goal was to produce a concise, bulleted, easy-to-understand, vision-like, one-page document of how employees would work in partnership.

For example, one of the bullets might be nothing more than, "If we have issues, we discuss them openly and honestly," or "We celebrate victories large and small." Typically, the HWWT would have no more than 10-15 bullets on a single page document. The idea behind this document was to capture the major points that would help teams be most successful.

All employees would be given a printed copy they would place at their desks to be reminded how they should work collaboratively as part of that team. If team members decided that changes or additions needed to be made to this document, they would discuss and agree unanimously before any changes would be made. This was *their* document, which created strong ownership among employees.

The second process, WWS, was a method for capturing quickly and concisely the major points of every meeting, which could be saved in an electronic document. Essentially, the WWS was nothing more than meeting minutes in a very short format with all decision and action items communicated clearly. For example, after a meeting with one of my executives, whether it was in-person or via teleconference, I would type up a WWS document that I would immediately email to him or her. If I forgot something in the document or misunderstood what was decided, it was the employee's responsibility to let me know immediately so I could make the change and email a new, corrected document.

The WWS document would be titled and saved as "WWS021510" signifying that the "What Was Said" meeting was held on February 15, 2010. This made it very easy to find notes for any and all meetings in which decisions were made.

For example, the simple document might read:

WWS 2/15/10

Randy D. Shillingburg

JT to submit sales numbers to Randy by 2/22
Randy to call Brian to ask question about new sales process
Randy to get back to JT by 2/24 with answer
JT given approval to hire new employee

We have all attended meetings in which something was decided and later a person attending the meeting would say, "We never decided that!"

This document, which required no more than a minute or two to type after a meeting and was sent via email, helped to ensure that major decisions and action items were never forgotten or overlooked. If something was decided, we had an electronic record by saving the dated WWS document.

Process is *vitally* important in any organization. These are just two quick process ideas you can use to improve communication and collaboration within your team!

△ △ △

I recently started watching "The Profit," a television show in which multi-millionaire Marcus Lemonis invests in small businesses all over America and then helps them focus on improving their products and processes, while ensuring they have the right people leading and working at these companies. I thoroughly enjoy watching this show and learn something new in nearly every episode. One day it dawned on me that his approach with small businesses all over America is very similar to how I provided executive oversight for my teams across the country.

While working with and doing consulting work for dozens of organizations of all sizes – from small non-profits to Fortune 500 companies – I've noticed that the most successful organizations always focus on ensuring they've developed processes for nearly everything – and training employees to follow those processes.

The teams I managed at College Summit never faltered, possibly because I helped them to focus on improving and even perfecting all of the processes that would drive their success.

While nearly every major community in America suffered through an economic recession following the housing bust of 2009, my sales teams in major cities experienced average annual growth in sales revenues of over 60 percent. Not many organizations in *any* market sector could boast of this level of financial success at that time, but then again, few organizations invested the same amount of time and effort to be successful as my teams did each and every month.

I have to believe that even Mr. Lemonis would have been impressed with the level of growth those teams were able to achieve by working together and perfecting the processes that would ensure their success.

Peak Performance Chapter Activities:

1) How detailed are the processes within your organization?
2) Do your processes vary significantly from employee to employee, location to location?
3) If so, why?
4) Do these variances enhance or inhibit growth?
5) What processes need improved and how can you improve or simplify them?
6) How can you improve how best practices are shared throughout your organization?
7) How can you utilize HWWT or WWS to improve communication and teamwork within your organization?

Chapter 19: Celebrating Victories, Large and Small

As humans, we crave positive attention. We want to be appreciated, and we want to be successful.

One of the many important things I've learned about quality, effective management is the importance of celebrating victories, large and small. Everyone wants to be successful, and everyone wants to be part of a winning team. Celebrations provide team members with the opportunity to feel as though they are a part of something bigger – and something very successful.

When I managed one-half of a large customer service center, I would often slap a $1 bill on the desk of the person on my side of the floor who would make the first sale in the morning. As soft drinks in our vending machines cost $1, essentially I was "buying a (name of soft drink)" for the person who completed the first transaction of the day. This may seem like something insignificant, but it created competition, excitement and a sense that we were a successful team. As I placed the dollar on the desk, I typically would also give the customer service representative a high five. Invariably, the next few people to complete a sale would raise their hands, and I would also give those people a celebratory high five – and sometimes I would buy them a soft drink, too.

We made work fun – not mundane.

When I managed the College Summit West Virginia office, we would often celebrate a sale to a school district or the receipt of a philanthropic gift with a team lunch at our favorite local restaurant, or even just an announcement before the entire team and a round of applause. When I managed sales teams in cities across America for College Summit, I would encourage my teams to celebrate victories, whether it was a school sale, a large philanthropic gift or improved college enrollment data because of their hard work.

When I coached my elementary basketball team, I would praise players when they did anything the correct way, even if they were just using the backboard to make shots when shooting close to the basket or deflecting a pass because they kept their hands raised on defense. I realized, even at an early age, that positive reinforcement works!

While coaching in one game, the youngest and smallest player on my team was passed the ball and was quickly tied up by a player on another team. The referee called for a jump ball. I actually praised the player from the sidelines, yelling "Great job! You got a jump ball!!" Other team members chimed in, too. The fourth grader's face beamed with pride with an ear-to-ear smile. I wanted this very young player, who was just starting to learn the game, to feel positive about himself and his role on the team.

△ △ △

As humans, we crave positive attention. We want to be appreciated, and want to be successful. If you're a parent, you know that if you say "Good job!" to one of your children you will always see a huge smile. And as an adult who was once a child, you know how much these two words meant when you heard them from your parents.

Saying "Good job," costs nothing, but it means the world to employees. Giving an employee a high five is essentially saying, "Good job," with the added measure of "I appreciate you" and "I am celebrating *your* success!"

I vividly remember an all staff conference that I attended with my talented and very dedicated College Summit colleagues from all over the country. After a particularly long training session, all of the employees were instructed to walk across the hall to a hotel banquet room for refreshments during a break.

We were completely surprised to find that banquet tables spaced throughout the room were filled with all of the treats we enjoyed as children at a carnival – from candy apples, to popcorn, snow cones, corn dogs, hot dogs, cotton candy, ice cream and even boxes of Cracker Jack! My fellow employees and I were transformed into children once more – with huge smiles on our faces as we were taken back to a time when we didn't have a care in the world.

I remember observing our CEO and Founder, J.B. Schramm, as he enjoyed one of those snacks. I'm not even sure what J.B. was eating, but he was thoroughly enjoying it! J.B. is one of the world's leaders on social change and had been a participant at the World Economic Forum in Davos, Switzerland, but at that moment he was once again just one very happy 10-year-old boy!

When I looked across the room at *all* of my wonderful, talented colleagues from across the country, I saw unbridled joy!

△ △ △

While with one organization years ago, I flew to Los Angeles to receive my performance review. Not only was I provided an outstanding review by two executives, but I was also awarded a financial bonus for my work. Needless to say, I was ecstatic. That afternoon, while walking through Hollywood, I gazed across the street and spotted a rental car lot that featured premium vehicles.

A cherry red Mustang caught my eye. I decided that I would celebrate!

I rented the Mustang for the day and drove it through Hollywood to Brentwood and all the way to the coast. I then headed up the Pacific Coast Highway to Malibu with warm coastal breezes blowing in my face. I drove the muscle car back to Hollywood and cruised down the Sunset Strip. I had an absolute blast in that high-performance Mustang! While I normally enjoy team celebrations much more than doing something by myself, I have to say that this was the one time I gave myself permission to revel in personal success by doing something very spontaneous.

△ △ △

As I have traveled the country and worked with organizations of all sizes, I've been amazed at how the most successful teams always seem to be the ones that regularly carve out a little time from their day-to-day work to celebrate victories, large and small. Whether doing consulting work with a world-wide chemical company in Hope, Arkansas, or Missoula, Montana, or with a great, locally-owned HVAC company in Morgantown, West Virginia, I have seen that the most successful teams purposefully take time away from their busy schedules to celebrate achievements and to enjoy camaraderie among team members.

The celebrations I have seen in various organizations across the country range from a quick team lunch or dinner, an afternoon activity such as going to the movies, a barbeque for employees and their families, a Christmas party, a Saturday evening themed dance with a live band, or a quick recognition at a staff or employee meeting. A few of these celebrations cost little to nothing, while a few easily cost tens of thousands.

Celebration doesn't have to cost a lot of money or require significant time away from work, but it is vitally important for team morale and team building.

While leading the College Summit West Virginia team, I developed a very simple certificate program to recognize employees for doing something positive during their day-to-day work. It was called the "Soaring Chicken Award" and could be given at any time by anyone on our team, but was typically presented at a morning staff meeting. Yes, it was a little off-beat, but it was also fun and employees looked forward to receiving and presenting the simple black and white certificate.

I always viewed this certificate as a perfect metaphor for our team of underdogs. No one really expected us to take off, but we *soared!*

Take the time to celebrate *your* team's success!

Peak Performance Chapter Activities:

1) Does your organization celebrate successes, large and small?
2) When was the last time your team or organization celebrated an achievement?
3) How can you do a more effective job of celebrating successes, large and small, in your organization?
4) How do your employees collectively and individually like to celebrate?

Chapter 20: Feedback

I learned that honest feedback is a great gift, if it is received from someone who sincerely only wants the best for you and the organization.

One of the greatest gifts any manager, executive or employee can receive is honest feedback. Any truly great organization has invested the time and effort to create a culture of feedback.

I remember receiving some valuable input from College Summit's CEO and Founder, J.B. Schramm, after a successful sales meeting we had attended together a few months after I started working with the organization.

"Randy, are you at a place where you can accept some feedback," this social change visionary asked me.

"Of course," I said.

"I'm not sure if the information I receive from you is 100% accurate," he said. "You always make it sound as if everything is great, but I know you've faced challenges. How are we going to learn what challenges you face and how to resolve them if all we hear is that everything is going well. As an organization, we want to learn and share with other teams what you've learned, and at other times, it might be better if we figure out what to do as an organization. How can we do this if you don't share your challenges with us?"

I have to admit that that his feedback hurt a little – at first. I was in the process of building what I believed would be the strongest, most effective team in the entire organization, and I was receiving what I initially perceived as negative feedback about my performance.

I considered his input over the next couple of days and realized that he was absolutely right. His feedback was a wonderful gift that helped me to become a better manager within our relatively new and fast-growing organization. Starting out in the corporate world, I had been trained to find *solutions* and not to bring *problems* to my boss. But when you're trying to build something new, whether in a for-profit business or a non-profit organization, you have to learn together – successes and failures.

I learned a lot from J.B. that day –and on many other days. He helped me to understand the importance of sharing in an organization that was expanding rapidly and learning as it grew.

△ △ △

Later, while leading my College Summit West Virginia team, and then teams in major cities all over the U.S., I encouraged my employees to provide honest feedback. I often asked what I could do better as their manager, because I truly wanted to be their best, most effective manager.

Whenever J.B., Brian Gaines or other executives from our national office would visit my teams, I would purposefully leave the office so they could meet privately with employees. I wanted employees to feel comfortable providing feedback about our organization and my performance to another leader within College Summit, if for any reason they didn't feel comfortable giving honest feedback directly to me.

I learned that feedback is a great gift, if it is received from someone who sincerely only wants the best for you and the organization. Just as with any gift, it can be accepted and appreciated, or it can be thrown away and forgotten. As I have worked across the country, I have seen that the top-performing organizations encourage feedback because they realize that it is a vital tool they can utilize to help them reach their full potential.

Randy D. Shillingburg

△ △ △

The executive in state government that I mentioned in a previous chapter strongly *discouraged* a culture of feedback. Through intimidating and even somewhat threatening communications and actions, he actually encouraged managers and employees to *not* be truthful about the challenges the organization faced as a result of his ill-informed decision.

Sadly, he was unwilling to accept any feedback or input whatsoever, even though managers and employees working under him cared deeply about their organization and its work – and even cared about this executive and wanted him to succeed – until he completely disrespected them. By not accepting feedback or input in any way, shape or form, he essentially *angrily* snatched a wonderful present from the hands of his employees and threw it in the garbage in front of them.

Whatever relationships this executive had with his managers were completely ruined, my friend told me. Whatever respect he had fostered with his employees over the years was completely thrown away, just as he tossed away his managers' gift of feedback.

Have you read the children's book, "Emperor's New Clothes," the Hans Christian Anderson classic in which subjects are afraid to tell the Emperor that he isn't wearing any clothes – so they keep telling him his clothes are beautiful? I can't think of a simpler, more appropriate description for this style of management. Thankfully, I have seen this style of leadership in only a few organizations I've worked with during my career.

These organizations never seem to reach their full potential. They are consistently being held by their own lack of candid feedback, which is a tool that should be used to make them stronger and more efficient.

Unless you are able and willing to confront issues honestly, you will never become a great organization or a truly effective manager. By hiring only people who will agree with you; by listening to only those people who think the same way as you think; or by discouraging open, honest communication; you may become the "emperor" of your subjects, but those subjects will never be candid with you about your true lack of "clothes" and your organization will never become great.

In essence, by hiring only people just like you, you are stacking your team with all of the same type of people. The diversity of viewpoints and talents on a team is what makes a group of individuals great – and stronger than the sum of its parts.

Imagine a basketball team with only short, quick guards, or only 7-foot centers. Neither would be a "winning" team. Any successful team requires different skill sets *and* mindsets!

△ △ △

If you manage an organization with multiple layers of management between you and your employees, I strongly encourage you to occasionally conduct meetings with employees to provide them with the opportunity to provide candid feedback. I also suggest that you encourage management working between them and you to leave the room so that employees aren't intimidated or discouraged from giving honest input – if you have any sense whatsoever that employees may be afraid to speak frankly.

Time and time again, in organizations of all sizes, I have seen the transformational impact of unfiltered feedback, as I have worked as an executive, manager and consultant. It's remarkable what organizations can learn about their processes, products and even the quality of their management – if leaders will only invest the time to ask for input and then listen to it.

I have to caution you, though, *before* you schedule any meeting with employees who do not report directly to you.

Before conducting *any* meetings with employees without your managers present, I *strongly* recommend that you communicate with management working under you to let them know why and when you are planning to meet with employees, so they aren't blindsided. Even the most effective managers may feel betrayed by executives or managers who discuss issues with their employees without talking with them first.

I have seen this typically-innocent oversight on several occasions during my career, and it *never* results in an organization becoming stronger or more effective, which is the ultimate goal of unfiltered feedback. The last thing you ever want as a leader is to have managers working under you who don't trust you or your motives, or wonder if you trust them to do their jobs. The few seconds it takes to inform managers working under you that you will be talking with their employees can eliminate *hours* later spent combating hurt feelings, changing employee *misconceptions* and rebuilding trust with your managers.

While creating a culture of feedback is vitally important for any organization, it is just as imperative to follow up on any feedback. While every suggestion can't be acted upon by leadership, employees should be told why their suggestions couldn't be enacted – but they should also be sincerely thanked for their input. When employee suggestions and feedback are implemented by any organization, employees should be informed and recognized/rewarded, especially if their input results in cost savings and greater efficiency.

Managers who are doing an effective job leading their employees won't ever be afraid for anyone working above them to receive feedback, as long as they learn about it before the fact, not after. I have also discovered that the top-performing managers in any organization will always welcome constructive criticism that can help them to become better, more effective leaders.

△ △ △

In addition to feedback from employees, I have found that the leading organizations in any market sector also seek input from other groups that are also vitally important – clients, customers and stakeholders.

One of the most eye-opening experiences earlier in my career was watching a focus group of customers while working with North Carolina Power/Virginia Power. We were starting the process of rolling out a new program for customers and wanted to understand how the average customer might react. A group of 15 customers was invited to a local hotel to participate in the focus group, which was conducted in a conference room over a two-hour period in the evening.

The focus group was conducted by an impartial, third-party consultant, who helped to ensure that customers would feel very comfortable providing candid feedback. While the facilitator asked questions and encouraged participation by all customers on the panel, a couple members of our management team watched via closed-circuit television in an adjacent room. I vividly remember walking away from the experience realizing that we could do a much better job with some of our customer interactions (we weren't as good as we thought we were) and that with only two or three minor tweaks the new program would be very well-received by our customers.

I have participated in only two other focus groups during my career, once as an observer for an organization and the other as the facilitator for a focus group. In each of those cases, just as in my first focus group experience with the utility company, I was a surprised at the clear disconnect between what managers in the organizations thought the average customer or stakeholder felt and believed – and what customers/ stakeholders clearly communicated as members of the focus groups.

During my career, I have utilized a number of other methods to ensure that organizations could receive regular feedback from their customers, clients and stakeholders – from Community Advisory Panels (CAPs), which I have formed and facilitated for Fortune 500 companies in various locations across the country; customer opinion surveys, which I have utilized with organizations of all sizes and in all market sectors; and social media, which can provide near instantaneous feedback through reviews, recommendations and comments.

CAPs are extremely effective in improving overall public perception for companies and creating a greater level of understanding among company representatives and community leaders for large, industrial corporations that otherwise struggle to connect with their communities. These are nothing more than third-party facilitated, structured meetings among company and key community leaders with well-established ground rules. The first such panel I formed was with North Carolina Power/Virginia Power in 1984, so my experience with CAPs dates back 35 years. Since then, I have formed or facilitated CAPs for corporations in numerous locations across the country – from Missoula, Montana, to Shippingport, Pennsylvania, and several locations in between.

Customer opinion surveys can provide strategic feedback to organizations of all sizes. Whether provided to customers at the time of sale, emailed/mailed to customers immediately after the experience, or emailed/mailed to a cross section of customers once a year, these surveys can provide valuable insight about the quality of service being provided to customers or clients. Nearly every organization I've worked with or have done consulting work for has used customer opinion surveys to assess quality of service or overall satisfaction levels.

Social media now provides every organization, no matter how large or small, with the opportunity to receive immediate feedback and to communicate directly with customers about their experiences. Today, social media has become crucially important, as about one out of every five internet page views (any internet page opened on a phone, tablet or computer) in America is on Facebook. Many organizations are ill-equipped and poorly-trained to use this relatively new communications vehicle to their greatest advantage. The fact is that social media can quickly and very inexpensively transform a company no one knows about into a community sensation in a matter of just a few months.

Feedback from customers is fundamentally important to managers and executives because it can help them to determine which employees are providing quality service and which ones aren't; and which teams are consistently performing at a high level and which ones aren't. Customer feedback is an integral tool you should utilize to lead your organization to improved performance.

Without exception, I've seen during my career that the most successful and consistently top-performing organizations in any market sector work very hard at receiving regular, candid feedback from employees, customers, clients and stakeholders – and then utilize this valuable insight to help them manage their teams to improved performance.

Peak Performance Chapter Activities:

1) Do one or two employees dominate the conversation at your meetings?
2) Are your employees encouraged or discouraged to discuss issues and to voice their opinions?
3) Do employees feel intimidated to speak up during meetings?
4) What can you do to encourage participation by all?
5) What can you do better to encourage a culture of feedback within your organization?
6) Does your organization confront or hide the issues that can help it improve?
7) What can you do to ensure more unfiltered feedback is received by executives and managers in your organization?
8) How can your organization do a better job of encouraging and listening to feedback from customers, clients and stakeholders?
9) Does your organization do an effective job of following up on feedback?
10) If you answered "No" to the previous question, how can your organization's follow-up be improved?

Chapter 21: Organizational Health

If all of these attributes are present in an organization, it will be successful no matter what the economy might bring.

All of the previous chapters discuss ways that managers can create a strong, healthy work environment.

ealthy organization is one in which a clear vision is understood, believed and even felt in all daily interactions among employees and customers or clients; the talents of employees are fully utilized; team members understand their responsibilities and are given the freedom to do their jobs without being micromanaged; goal-setting and performance reviews are more like collaborative conversations than stress-filled, once-a-year meetings; a culture has been created throughout the organization that encourages open, honest communication and feedback; decision rights are delineated and understood, with most day-to-day decisions *driven down* in the organization to the lowest possible level; celebrating success is a principal component of the organization's culture; new employees are brought on board purposefully and with a systemic effort to instill the same culture with each new hire; and employees are managed in a way that makes them feel inspired, challenged and appreciated.

I have seen that when all of these attributes are present, any organization will be successful no matter what the economy might bring. Employees will enjoy their work and look forward to coming to the office or facility every single day. I have also seen on numerous occasions that if even one of these attributes is lacking, the organization will falter short-term or long-term.

When I walk into an office of a small business, a large corporation, government agency or even a non-profit organization, I can typically tell within 10-15 minutes if the organization is healthy or shows signs of being very unhealthy. An unanswered phone, a negative comment about a manager or employee, employees grumbling about management or my learning about a key employee finding another job are clear signs that the organization's health may be less-than-healthy.

Having worked with so many different types of organizations, I have almost a sixth sense about what may be occurring within any office. After just a few minutes in any facility, or by directing a couple of questions to an employee or manager, I can usually gain a lot of insight about an organization's overall health.

△ △ △

Several years ago, I developed a simple and quick activity to assess overall organizational health. To test this activity, I asked members of a company's management team to rate their individual *professional* happiness within that organization. I asked each manager to place a number between "1" and "5" on a slip of paper, with the following instructions:

- A "1" will signify that you are very unhappy and actively searching for other employment.
- A "2" will signal unhappiness, too, and that you would quickly leave if you found another opportunity with even the same pay or benefits.
- A "3" will mean that you aren't necessarily extremely happy or unhappy, but would likely leave if given another opportunity with a little more money or better benefits.
- A "4" will signify that you are happy, and likely would not leave for another job, even if offered more money or better benefits.
- Lastly, a "5"will mean that you are *very* happy at the company and probably would not leave for another job even if you are offered more compensation or better benefits.

After collecting each slip of folded paper so that members of the management team could not see who had written which number, I wrote down the data I had collected. With each leader rating their level of satisfaction, I didn't receive a single "4." Numbers ranged from "2" to "3," with the vast majority being only "2s." The average of all ratings was only 2.3.

The health of this organization was absolutely horrible. If the leadership of this company was this dissatisfied, how would the average employee rate his or her satisfaction? Think about it – the management of this company was unhappy and the majority would leave if given another opportunity with even the same pay and benefits!

Conversely, I have facilitated this same activity with a few other organizations and have received nearly all 4s and 5s, which signals that employees or managers are extremely happy and the organization is healthy. The organizations with this high level of satisfaction among managers and employees will *consistently* outperform those with significantly lower averages. I've seen time and time again that those with the strongest organizational health are *always* market leaders.

People who are happy in their current roles, challenged, appreciated and given the authority to do their jobs aren't searching for other employment. Human beings inherently don't enjoy or welcome change – unless their current situation is depressing or unchallenging – or they feel unappreciated and clearly aren't happy.

How healthy is your organization or team under *your* leadership?

Peak Performance Chapter Activities:

1) Facilitate the organizational health activity described in this chapter for your managers or employees.
2) Ensure that your direct reports can rank their level of happiness in their roles anonymously and without repercussions.
3) Add up all of your numbers and divide the total by the number of employees submitting their ratings.
4) If your average is 3 or lower, organizational health needs some work and you should determine why your employees aren't happier.
5) If your average is 4 or above, organizational health is very good.
6) Even if your organizational health is great, what can you do better?

Chapter 22: Responsibility vs. Authority

Whether in the goal-setting process or just completing day-to-day activities, employees want to feel as though they are a vital part of the organization's success.

A few months after starting work at College Summit, several managers, executives and I had a discussion about what we called "responsibility vs. authority."

A few of us had the ultimate responsibility for growing our regions, but we lacked the clear authority to make the decisions that would allow us to thrive. In other words, we faced the consequences for not meeting goals, but a few of the major decisions related to achieving those goals were completely out of our hands or controlled by others.

Our discussion prompted a major reorganization, which resulted in stronger, more consistent growth within College Summit because those of us who had the responsibility of growing our regions were then also given more authority to make the decisions that affected our growth. I've always remembered that discussion and have seen the impact of this disconnect between responsibility and authority many times during my career.

I look back and realize that my greatest source of frustration professionally was when I was held accountable for achieving goals, but wasn't given the flexibility or even the authority to determine how to meet them. There is nothing more frustrating to a manager or employee than being held accountable for reaching goals, but also being told *exactly* how to achieve them, every step of the way.

Imagine feeling extreme pressure to achieve goals, but being told how to manage your staff, who to hire, when to hire employees even when you have open positions, how to complete your work, how to utilize your staff to complete the work and even how to manage your supervisors. Sadly, I've seen this style of leadership in a few organizations, which results in utter frustration and eventually a mass exodus of managers – or completely-defeated managers who simply wait to be told what to do and when to do it because they can't make a single decision without being second-guessed.

In a nutshell, this is responsibility with no authority.

No matter what organization I've worked with across the country, I have seen the same frustration among managers and employees when they are given responsibility without also being given the authority. In every instance, I've seen little employee buy-in. In a couple of instances, I have actually watched as key employees sabotaged management efforts because they had no control whatsoever – except to determine whether or not management's initiatives were successes or complete failures.

Whether in the goal-setting process or just performing day-to-day activities, employees want to feel as though they are a vital part of the organization's success. Just as my father taught me years ago, employees don't want to be told what to do, when to do it and how to do it – and then be held accountable when the work isn't done correctly.

If you have the responsibility for meeting goals, you should also have the authority to determine the vast majority of decisions that will allow you to achieve them.

Peak Performance Chapter Activities:

1) List three responsibilities or goals for at least one of your employees.
2) For each responsibility or goal list three or four major decisions necessary for that employee to achieve his or her goals.

3) Are any of these decisions out of your employee's control?
4) How can you provide all of your employees or managers with more authority to make the decisions necessary to reach their goals since, ultimately, it is *their* responsibility to achieve them?
5) Do you feel that any of your organization's decisions have been sabotaged by employees or other managers?
6) Why do you believe this occurred?

Chapter 23: No Limits

While a few may start out a little higher up on the rung of life than the rest of us, we all live in a country where anybody from anywhere can accomplish nearly anything through hard work and a positive attitude.

Another important lesson I've learned during my career and life is that we limit ourselves significantly more than others ever limit us. Nothing will ever hold us back more than our own thoughts, actions and attitudes.

At age five, in 1963, I survived what was then experimental open heart surgery to correct a congenital valve defect that prevented sufficient oxygen from being transported from my heart through my blood stream. I was what they called a "blue baby." Without this life-saving surgery, I would have died in my teens or would have lived a life with a lot of physical restrictions.

I still hazily remember my heart surgeon pulling me out of a wheelchair by my ears the day after surgery, telling me that there was no reason whatsoever why I shouldn't be walking up and down the halls following the life-changing operation.

I recall that event now and strongly believe that this was a pivotal point in my life that helped shape who I became. The doctor told me – no, he made me – not to feel sorry for myself and to push myself more than my family and I originally thought I should.

Once I received the magical words of "no restrictions" from my doctor after I reached puberty and had a second heart catheterization to ensure the surgery was a success, I began lifting weights to become stronger. During my lifetime, I've benched pressed as much as 350 pounds (at age 55), swum as far as two and one-half miles and have run up to 15 miles. At age 60, I still lift weights regularly, and recently bench pressed 320 pounds one rep and 225 pounds 18 times. To put this in perspective, the second pick in the NFL Draft a few years ago – a gigantic defensive tackle – bench pressed 225 pounds 22 times.

I'm not a large person, but I have trained my body to achieve close to its peak performance.

Just as we can limit ourselves physically, we can also restrict our own professional trajectory because of our socio-economic background. That, too, is a huge mistake.

Like so many others, I grew up in what most would consider to be a relatively poor family – in an economically-challenged area of West Virginia, Preston County. Our family didn't have a lot, but we were never hungry. There were families in our community a lot poorer, but there were also those who had a lot more than we did.

I have never used my heart surgery or upbringing as an excuse not to succeed. If anything, I have used each challenge as motivation and even a source of pride.

△ △ △

Did you know that the song, "Yankee Doodle" was originally written by the British as an insult to the American colonists?

If you really think about the lyrics we sang so many times as kids, you can *feel* the sarcasm.

"Yankee Doodle" was another way of saying "country bumpkin." He rode into town on a pony, which was most likely a filthy farm pony – not a majestic horse like the British owned. And when this bumpkin stuck a feather in his cap, he called it "macaroni," which meant "high fashion" at the time of the Revolutionary War. By sticking a feather in his hat, even though his clothes may have been ragged and dirty, this country bumpkin thought he was dressing up when he rode into town?

Yes, this was clearly an insult to the Americans. The colonists had the last laugh, though.

As the British soldiers laid down their arms in surrender at Yorktown, Virginia, what song did the Americans have played?

"Yankee Doodle."

I've shared this story numerous times as I have given speeches and presentations all over the country. The moral of this interesting tidbit of history is that you can consider your challenges and obstacles either as excuses to fail, or as extra motivation, driving you to succeed.

I've always chosen the latter.

△ △ △

Imagine growing in Tunnelton, and then later managing executives across the country; speaking at regional and national conferences; meeting with school, civic and corporate leaders in America's largest cities; and even training an executive in the middle of New York City.

I feel blessed to have achieved all that I have, but I also realize that my parents, especially my mother, Betty, made me believe as a child that I should experience a life of "no limits."

My father provided me with a strong work ethic and taught me persistence. He was the Scoutmaster for Troop 90 and strongly encouraged me to become an Eagle Scout, which took five years of hard work to achieve. While many kids in my community may have been watching cartoons on Saturday mornings, my dad and I were clearing brush on our family's small farm, except for when it was raining so hard we couldn't work outside.

As a teenager, I was much like the young people that College Summit supported in communities all over America, students whose parents didn't have the knowledge or experience to help their children find their way to college. Neither of my parents even graduated from high school. They had both dropped out to help their families put food on the table during the Great Depression.

Randy D. Shillingburg

I lost my mother at 16, a few months after receiving my Eagle Scout award, and my father died when I was only 19. Seeing my mom dying of a heart attack when I came home from school on February 20, 1975, and then watching my dad waste away from colon cancer for the next three years made me grow up fast and become fiercely independent. I didn't have them in my life long enough, but I am thankful that I had two wonderful, caring parents for as long as I did.

By the time I was ready to graduate from high school, my mother had already passed away and my father was slowly dying. I have to admit that my last year and a half of high school was a complete blur of being home alone, visiting my dad in the hospital and worrying about what my future might bring. Clearly, I was still in shock after losing one parent and seeing the other one dying steadily before my eyes.

I'm not exactly sure how I even made it to college, except for the grace of God and the strong belief my mother had instilled in me at an early age that I *should* further my education.

After sitting out a year following high school, I somehow found my way to Fairmont State, studied journalism, and was named editor of our college newspaper, "The Columns," by our very dedicated journalism professor/newspaper advisor, Jane Dumire. This professor/mentor asked me to lead the weekly publication during my entire junior year, selecting me over students from much larger high schools in West Virginia and from other states. I'm not exactly sure how or why she picked me for this leadership role, but she apparently saw some unrealized potential in a very long-haired, but rough-around-the-edges young man from Preston County.

Furthering my education at Fairmont State *completely* changed my life, providing me with career opportunities I never thought would have been possible.

△ △ △

I fondly remember the first time I visited the Jefferson Hotel in downtown Richmond, Virginia, with its ornate marble, huge three-story staircase and beautiful crystal ballroom chandeliers the size of small houses. I had just started working at North Carolina Power/Virginia Power in 1984 and was attending my first major corporate conference, helping to develop and implement the utility's new employee volunteer program. I walked through that historic hotel with my mouth gaped wide open because I had never seen such a beautiful place.

Two decades later, I'm flying on planes nearly every week in order to work with executives across the country and later doing consulting work in Montana, Arkansas, Texas, Florida, Pennsylvania and New Jersey with several of the largest corporations in the world. I'm driving in major cities such as Los Angeles and Miami, training an executive in Manhattan and corporate managers from Belgium, Spain, Thailand and other countries from around the world. From time to time, I had to pinch myself, not truly believing where I was or what I was doing.

In my mind, I've *never* been anything more than a kid from Preston County.

I still remember the first time I was upgraded free to a seat in First Class on a US Airways flight because I had earned "Silver Status." I heard the announcement over the loudspeaker that the available meal was a chicken sandwich.

When the flight attendant asked me what I wanted to order for lunch, I told her I would like to have the Chicken Ciabatta sandwich that had been announced over the loudspeaker as the available meal.

"Oh, no, Mr. Shillingburg, that sandwich is for those back *there*, in coach," she said as she motioned somewhat dismissively to the passengers sitting behind the curtain in coach. "We have a *special* meal for you."

She offered me a choice. I chose the "Chicken Mediterranean" option, which included a hot roll, chicken and pasta, salad and warm cookies for desert. Everything was served on porcelain dinnerware, with real silverware and a cloth napkin.

I have to admit that although I enjoyed the upgrades and perks that came with flying so frequently, I also felt very guilty because I never felt quite as important as the other people sitting in First Class. Growing up, it was a very special treat to eat at a fast food restaurant – or any restaurant for that matter. The definition of "elite" for me was going out to dinner at the Four Corners Restaurant in Grafton, West Virginia, once every few months with my parents. I certainly knew that the only difference between my seat in first class and the very last seat at the back of the plane was the amount of time I had spent traveling on airplanes in previous months.

I could almost write another book based on my experiences while traveling, from sitting in First Class behind Jane Seymour and then directing her and her assistant to ground transportation; to sitting across from the famous wrestler, Nature Boy Rick Flair, on a flight from Los Angeles; sitting beside and conversing with NFL quarterback Chad Pennington on a flight; talking with actress Connie Britton for 20 minutes outside a restaurant while I was in Austin, Texas, for a conference; meeting and talking with actor Don Cheadle at a College Summit "all staff" conference; and even sitting beside an Abraham Lincoln impersonator on a flight when he was on his way back home after reciting the Gettysburg Address on C-Span. Yes, he looked *exactly* like President Lincoln!

Probably the funniest story, though, was my first trip to the west coast to begin supporting a College Summit executive, Alexis Shah, and her team in Los Angeles. Before I left, employees in West Virginia told me to keep an eye out for celebrities, so, using my phone, I took a picture of an elderly couple waiting for a flight at LAX. They definitely weren't celebrities.

I was in the process of texting my employees a picture and jokingly telling them that I had snapped a photo of Brad Pitt and Angelina Jolie, when actor James Caan of "The Godfather" walked directly in front of me, no more than two feet away.

No, I never took *his* picture. I was too dumbfounded at seeing a *real* celebrity.

△ △ △

Immediately before the flight attendant closed the door on a small plane headed to Charleston, West Virginia, late one spring several years ago, I watched as a tall, blonde-haired younger man rushed onto the plane. I was saddened to think that I might soon have someone with very long legs sitting beside me in the open seat on my final flight home from a tiring West Coast trip. The last-minute passenger squeezed through the narrow aisle, made his way back through the plane and, of course, sat down beside me.

He looked *very* familiar.

Almost immediately upon taking his seat, he took out a three-ringed binder from his backpack and began flipping through the pages, taking notes feverously. On the cover of the binder was printed in colorful, bold letters, "Miami Dolphins Quarterback Camp."

Now, I knew who he was. He was NFL quarterback Chad Pennington.

I didn't bother him as he worked, until we were about halfway into the flight.

"You're not very bright, are you?" I asked.

He quickly looked up from his binder and replied somewhat defensively, "What do you mean?"

"Chad, how many years have you been in the league?" I asked with a huge smile spreading across my face.

"Thirteen," he replied. "You still have to study because they add new plays and formations, and plays change from year to year." By now, he was smiling, too. He knew he was sitting beside a fan with a sense of humor.

"Chad, I've followed your career in college and the NFL, and I have never heard of you getting into any trouble or facing any controversy – not even once," I said.

"You know why that is, don't you?" he questioned.

"No I don't," I replied.

"Great parents."

I could easily see the sincere pride and deep love in his eyes as he talked about how his mom and dad tried their best to raise him the "right way."

I thoroughly enjoyed the rest of our conversation, which included more details about his parents, his time at Marshall University and a long, successful career in the NFL.

Over the years, I've thought a number of times about how admiringly Chad talked about his parents, and how fortunate I was to have wonderful parents, too.

While I certainly wish I would have had my mom and dad longer, I am very fortunate to have had two key guides early in my life that provided me with a very strong footing.

My attitude has always been to be grateful for what you have, not deeply remorseful for what you don't.

Randy D. Shillingburg

I'm sharing these anecdotes because when I was in my teens, I never thought in even my wildest dreams that I would have the opportunity to travel to so many different places, meet so many wonderful people and to work with dozens of truly great organizations as an employee and consultant. I have been unbelievably blessed to experience all that I've seen and done.

The world is full of achievers, many of whom begin their lives in very humble or even deeply troubled beginnings. I admire those who start out with very little, overcome numerous obstacles and make something of themselves, whether it's starting a successful small business, developing new products that change the world, building a great career working for someone else or providing their children with a supportive, loving home.

I have to admit that I am proudest when learning about successful West Virginians. We are a resilient, humble, hard-working group of people. No matter where we may end up, we share a common bond and great love for our beautiful state.

While traveling in a rental car van at LAX one afternoon several years ago, the only other passenger and I started talking. We both had a little bit of a "twang" in our voices. I learned that he was originally from Princeton, West Virginia, and that he still attended nearly every WVU football game. Later, while walking through the farmer's market in San Francisco, I started talking with a man walking a golden retriever and learned he also was from West Virginia, but was now living high up in the mountains of California. A West Virginia friend recently posted a video on Facebook of "Country Roads" being played at a bar in Australia, with all of the patrons proudly singing the unofficial state anthem.

We are everywhere!

Growing up as I did, I have always believed that the true measure of a person isn't how high up on the organization chart his or her name appears. The only accurate measures are how far a person has traveled to get to where he or she is today, and, most importantly, how he or she has treated others to get there.

I've also learned through the years that the only differences between those who succeed and those who don't are attitude, hard work, a belief in oneself, and a little luck.

While a few may start out a little higher up on the rung of life than the rest of us and face fewer obstacles, we all live in a country where *anybody* from *anywhere* can accomplish nearly *anything* through hard work and a positive attitude.

△ △ △

My first job after graduating from high school – before I attended college – was helping to wire coal cleaning plants in north central West Virginia.

I would arrive home with coal dirt around my eyes and embedded deep in the pores of my skin. I would sometimes need to take two or three showers just to get clean, because I would discover when I looked in the mirror after bathing that I hadn't scrubbed hard enough and wasn't thorough enough to remove *all* of the coal dirt and grime. Even though I believed I was dirt-free after multiple showers, I would need to wash my bed clothes every few days because I would see an outline of my body on the sheets, thanks to the coal dust that came out through my pores when I was sleeping.

While I was in college, I worked on repair jobs for coal power stations during the summer. This, too, was often very dirty work – and very hot. At one power station where I was working, company officials had placed a thermometer where we were working, which was beside a boiler burning coal to generate electricity. I remember seeing the thermometer at over 135 degrees one day. It felt like an oven, so much so that I actually developed goose pimples when I walked outside into 90-degree-plus temperatures. My body had become so accustomed to the extreme heat that I felt chilled when I walked outside because of the dramatic temperature change.

Perhaps because of the way I was raised and where I've worked, I know that I am no better than anyone else. I am not any more special than a construction worker, clerk at a convenience store, or the woman who works at WalMart. I have always treated the CEO of a major corporation with the same respect as the janitor at a small high school or the waitress at a local, family restaurant.

Many of the people I remember most fondly during my life are construction workers, custodians, waitresses, secretaries, clerks and fast food workers. Some of the most intelligent, greatest people I've met in my life are those unsung heroes who go to work every day, support their families and raise their children to have respect for others. My wife is somewhat surprised that nearly every employee at the Burger King in Bridgeport greets me by name – and I acknowledge them by their first names!

That's just how and who I am – and have always been. I'm a West Virginian through and through.

△ △ △

When I led the College Summit West Virginia team to unexpected success, I strongly believed that the group of people I managed was as talented and intelligent as any across the nation. I would venture a guess that very few in the entire organization believed that this group of people from West Virginia – all of whom had what some might say a "funny accent" – would become the first to prove a sophisticated business model developed by a few of the leading social entrepreneurs in America.

When I managed teams all over the country for College Summit to similar success, I had the same unwaveringly positive attitude about my teams. For me, it was truly an honor to manage and lead these wonderful, extremely talented people.

When I led professionals all over the country for a public relations firm as Director of Operations, I also had this same viewpoint – that I was so incredibly blessed to be supporting and managing extremely gifted, dedicated people, from the wonderful staff at our office to our talented professional consultants working in the field.

Becoming a great manager is nothing more than helping others to believe that they, too, have nearly unlimited potential. To achieve this, every once in a while you may have to give them a "kick in the butt" – just as the doctor did when he pulled me out of the wheelchair by my ears – but most of the time you inspire people to greatness through encouraging words and positive reinforcement.

Everyone has value.

My belief has always been that if your goal as a manager is to build a strong, sustainable organization that achieves peak performance, you should work every single day to find the inherent, untapped value in your employees, too.

Peak Performance Chapter Activities
1) List your employees.
2) Beside each employee's name, list the values they bring to your organization.
3) Take the time to understand more about your employees' backgrounds so that you can appreciate them more as people – not just employees.
4) What additional values can these employees bring to your organization, now that you know more about them?
5) What limits do you place on yourself that are preventing you from achieving greatness in your life or within your organization?
6) What limits do you unconsciously place on your employees that may be restricting their development?

Chapter 24: Inspired Leadership

Being a leader is bringing people together in a manner so they want to follow.

I enjoy listening to audio tapes and reading books by the late Wayne Dyer. I remember when I first heard Dyer talking about what it means to be "inspired." He explained that this word in essence means being "in spirit." In other words, when you feel most inspired, you are actually tapping into your spiritual side; you are living closer to God.

I believe that being a great manager isn't about demanding from others; it's about *inspiring* others to greatness.

No matter where I worked in the last half of my career, I would try to spend a few minutes every day just observing and listening, taking the time to be inspired by my employees. I would listen to the constant "buzz" of reps talking on the phone in the large customer service center, watch the friendly connections among my employees at a small business as they worked, or enjoy the positive interactions among corporate and community representatives as one of my employees at the public relations firm facilitated a meeting. No matter where I worked, I would enjoy just taking a few minutes to just sit, listen and enjoy the human connections.

After a few minutes, I might even imagine myself floating high above my employees, watching over them as they enjoyed their work. I tried to place myself on a "higher plane" spiritually for a few minutes each day so that I could truly enjoy and appreciate all that was occurring around me. I found that my heart rate would slow down and my blood pressure would drop because I was trying to live more "in the moment" than stressing about the work that had to be completed on that particular day.

I often enjoy this same exercise if I'm at a mall or even a park – take the time to appreciate and enjoy the human connections and interactions with nature. I know this may sound a little strange, but you should try it sometime. This exercise will bring you a sense of calm even during your worst days. Imagine the people and nature around you as something much more important than the here and now – part of something that is truly Godly.

Fernando Ibanez, the very talented webmaster I worked with at the West Virginia Department of Education, once told me that "Europeans work to live, while Americans live to work." Growing up in Spain, he saw how Europeans appreciate the human interactions through their daily work that enable them to experience happier, more fulfilled lives, while Americans are more consumed with the job and earning a living, making *this* the focus of their lives. As I've grown older, I've tried to do more of the former and much less of the latter.

Whenever I led or facilitated employee meetings in numerous organizations, I would often just sit back and listen as employees interacted, without saying a single word. If you're a true leader, you will thoroughly enjoy just watching the human connections among your employees, knowing that you have created a collaborative environment that encourages quality communications and decision-making. This is leadership operating on a different, much higher plane.

A large part of being a manager who works "in spirit" is realizing that even your best, most talented employees will have bad days or make mistakes. It doesn't mean that they aren't dedicated or lack intelligence; it means that they are human. And from time to time, you will need to realize that when an employee has a bad day, it may be because of a personal or family issue.

△ △ △

Many years ago, Billy Joe Wooten and I were having breakfast together. As the waitress walked by, my friend quietly said, "Randy, look at the pain in that woman's face."

My fellow manager at North Carolina Power/Virginia Power saw the frown and stress lines on this woman's human facade as well as the dullness in her eyes. He knew instinctively that she had lived a rough life.

Billy Joe was one of the smartest, most insightful people I've ever known. He had learned to look beyond the exterior to see people for who they truly are – and what they are experiencing.

△ △ △

Being a leader isn't about being the most intelligent, loudest, most animated person in the room, or the one with the longest or most prestigious title. In fact, Jim Collins discovered while doing the research for his "Good to Great" book that the most effective leaders aren't the ones who are the most dynamic. He found that the leaders who build the strongest, longest-lasting and consistently most profitable companies are the people who lead quietly and unassumingly.

I believe that being a leader isn't about *demanding* from others, but helping others become successful by inspiring them. Being a leader is bringing people together in such a manner that they *want* to follow.

As I have worked with organizations of all sizes and in all market sectors across the country for nearly four decades, what have I seen consistently in those leaders that employees enthusiastically follow?

The type of leaders others *want* to follow:

- Listen more than they talk
- Are enthusiastic and positive
- Invite input from all
- Make all feel as if they are part of something great
- Make the person they are talking with feel as though he or she is the most important person in the world
- Make all feel as though they are a vital part of the decision-making process

Compare these attributes to the type of leaders I have seen no one wants to follow:

- Talk more than they listen
- Are negative and unenthusiastic
- Rarely ask for input
- Make all feel insignificant
- Make the person they are talking with feel as though he or she is unimportant
- Make decisions themselves with little input from others

The mark of a great leader is that even without the prestigious title or the higher salary others would still follow. True leaders bring people together enthusiastically, make team members feel important, listen to their opinions and solicit input from all. True leaders produce calm in their teams, solicit knowledge from others, and create greater understanding and respect among those they work with every day.

Conversely, I have consistently seen that terrible, ineffective leaders generate stress, believe they know it all and create much more confusion than understanding.

What type of leader do you want to be – one that others want to follow, or one that others follow only because you are the boss?

Which type of leader do you think is operating more "in spirit," the one who listens and is very positive when interacting with others, or the leader who talks more than he or she listens and has a consistent, negative outlook?

△ △ △

My final thoughts in this chapter are that I have always felt blessed – and that I am so very thankful for all I have been given in this life, even life itself. I would like to share a little more about my life, including why I feel this way.

As I wrote in a previous chapter, I entered this world with a heart defect. What I didn't share earlier is that I was also born with a hole in my heart, which initially prevented me from having life-saving surgery.

I was too young to remember from first-hand experience what I'm about to share. This story, which has become part of our family lore, was told to me *numerous* times by my mother when she was still alive. If you ever met my mom, you would know she didn't exaggerate – not at all. She was about as "real" of a person you would ever meet.

At some point when I was several months old, our elderly, very religious next door neighbor, Carrie Taylor, walked over to our home to talk with my mom one morning.

"Betty," Carrie said joyfully, "Jesus came to me in a dream last night. I saw the hole in Randy's heart being filled in completely. It's gone! He's going to be all right and will be able to have his surgery."

A couple of days later, my mom and I traveled to see the heart surgeon in Morgantown, West Virginia, for a regularly-scheduled check-up. The doctor ordered tests to assess my condition and discovered that the void in my heart had completely disappeared, just as Carrie had told my mother. We could now move forward with the surgery that would ultimately save my life, once I became old enough and strong enough for the doctors to perform the operation.

Here's a second story that both my mother and oldest sister told me *numerous* times. In fact, my sister and I were talking about this incident just a month or so ago.

A few years after Carrie had her dream, I was extremely worried and nervous, as any five-year-old might be while anticipating a long hospital stay and open heart surgery. I was scheduled to travel to the University Hospital in Morgantown early the next morning for the operation.

Although I wasn't old enough to fully understand the inherent dangers I would be facing in the coming days, I was nervous and on edge because my family appeared to be very scared. Even young children can sense when something's wrong and family members are worried.

My oldest sister, Melodye, took a shower in our basement early that evening. After finishing her bath and getting dressed, she saw the pants legs and boots of a man standing partially down our basement stairs, his face and upper body hidden from view.

"Randy won't be having surgery this week," the man said.

After hearing these very few words, my sister saw the man turn and walk the rest of the way up the stairs, disappearing into the darkness. She never saw his face or recognized his voice.

Clearly startled, my sister nervously waited a minute or two. Not seeing the man reappear or anyone standing at the top of the stairs, she quickly ran upstairs to let our mom and dad know what she had just seen. Our parents explained to her that no one else had been in the house and that they hadn't opened the door to the basement or had gone downstairs. The door had been closed the entire time, they told her. Our parents undoubtedly believed that their oldest daughter was anxious about my surgery and may have *thought* she had seen or heard something.

Later that evening, mom received a phone call from the hospital. She was informed that my surgery had been postponed because the doctors thought I might have had the start of a cold when I had been at their offices earlier that week. They didn't want to take any chances, so I would not be checking into the hospital the next morning to prepare for the long and arduous operation.

My family and I were relieved. None of us was emotionally prepared for the surgery – at least not just yet. We all needed a little more time to prepare for the mental ordeal of very dangerous open heart surgery. Clearly, we all needed to get our "heads on straight" in order for the surgery to be successful.

While I was too young at the time to remember these incidents today, I have been told them many times by my mother and oldest sister. If they said these events occurred, they did.

These are just two of several unusual occurrences in my life that aren't easily explained – unless you have faith.

During my career, I have been presented *numerous* opportunities that I completed *kicking and screaming* – initially not wanting to do them at all – only to learn that what I was essentially *forced* into doing was necessary in order to have other, more significant opportunities that would advance my professional career.

For example, I wasn't interested in *anything* having to do with public education when North Carolina Power/Virginia Power was asked to participate in a study, "The Condition of Being an Educator," conducted by the Public School Forum of North Carolina in the mid-1980s. Our utility was one of a half dozen major corporations asked to provide representatives who would interview teachers and principals for this statewide research project.

Despite my objections that I was too busy to take time away from my regular duties with the power company, I was informed that I had been selected to be our company's representative for this study – and I *would* be participating.

This initial, very reluctant foray into public schools piqued my interest and helped me to develop strong community connections and key educational insights that were needed for me to take the next step – and many subsequent steps – in my long and winding career.

This initial experience in public education led me to develop a number of award-winning educational programs while with the utility company, which led to working with two public school systems and the West Virginia Department of Education, which led to managing school-business partnerships all across West Virginia, which led to leading a successful statewide non-profit and eventually to providing executive oversight for very talented teams all over America that helped *thousands* of low-income students enroll in college.

Although I could never see the winding path set before me at the times these opportunities were initially presented, I look back now and realize that these chances to learn and grow professionally were all part of a much larger, well-designed plan. I have no reasonable justification for this – or for the stories I shared with you earlier – other than I know with *100 percent certainty* that I have been watched over my entire life by a power much greater than I.

For this reason, I have always *strongly* believed that my life and work are blessings and that every day I have experienced on this Earth is a wonderful gift – the gift of life and yet another day. While most people take life or their daily employment for granted, I don't – and never have.

△ △ △

So I ask you once more, what type of manager do you want to be – the one who inspires employees, or the one who demands from, degrades and belittles those who work with you?

Do you want to be the person who leads his or her team to greatness, or the manager who settles for mediocrity?

Do you want to be the person employees enthusiastically follow and respect, or the manager others pay attention to only because you have the title?

Do you want to experience your next day leading others as a *wonderful* opportunity to make a difference in people's lives, or just another eight hours in an uninspired life?

It's all up to you!

Peak Performance Chapter Activities:

1) Write down the first set of bullets described in this chapter – the attributes of a leader others want to follow.
2) On a scale of 1 to 10, with 1 being the lowest possible rating and 10 being the highest possible rating, assess your performance for each of these attributes.
3) Ask your employees to rate you anonymously in each of the attributes.
4) How do your ratings differ from your employees'?
5) What areas do you need to improve on as a manager?
6) List one action item in each area needing improvement you will work on during the next month to become more of a leader others will want to follow.
7) Invest at least 15 minutes today just observing your employees, their interactions with customers or clients – and with each other.
8) What did you notice or learn?
9) How can you live your life and manage others more "in spirit?"
10) What is your "path?"

Randy D. Shillingburg

Chapter 25: Looking in the Mirror

Based on my experience with organizations of all sizes, I strongly believe these four attributes point to a single issue – ineffective leadership that inspires no one.

I have had the privilege and honor of working with a large number of organizations that were clear leaders in their fields. I've also had the opportunity to work with and do consulting work for a couple of organizations that always seemed to struggle. Sadly, a few of the managers in these organizations didn't have enough self-awareness to realize that they were the problem, not the employees who worked for them.

So, what are the signs that could indicate leadership is an issue in your organization – and that you may need to look a good, hard look in the mirror to see the root of the problem?

High employee turnover
Studies have consistently shown that most employees don't change jobs because of their duties, salaries or co-workers; they quit because of their bosses. When an organization experiences extreme turnover, this is a very strong indication that management is lacking. Most human resource experts conservatively estimate that the true cost of losing an employee is between one-third and one-half of that employee's annual salary.

An organization that loses even five employees with an average salary of $40,000 sees a true impact to its bottom line of between $67,000 and $100,000. If you are continually losing employees to other organizations, you might want to look in the mirror. You or your managers are likely the reason people are leaving. Employees typically don't leave organizations; they leave bosses they don't like.

Lack of sustained growth

Well-managed organizations always seem to improve performance year over year, while those with management issues have revenue graphs that look more like electrocardiograms – up and down. If your organization's performance is inconsistent year to year, you may have a leadership problem and the problem may be you or your managers.

Great leaders create a culture of striving for continuous improvement and true ownership that permeates throughout the entire organization. Quality leadership results in employees enthusiastically and diligently working together to beat last year's results – each and every year.

No one seems to be able to make a decision – except you

I have heard managers say, "No one else can make a decision," without realizing that they created this culture by second guessing or constantly overruling their employees' decisions. Employees empowered to make decisions have a strong sense of ownership in their jobs, while employees who are always second-guessed will eventually quit making decisions. I have seen this happen many times in numerous organizations of all sizes – hard-working, motivated employees who quit thinking for themselves and wait for their bosses to tell them what to do after a few months of being second-guessed. If your employees seemingly can't make quality decisions for your organization, it's probably because you or your managers have taught them *not* to make decisions.

Performance always seems to slip when management is out of the office

Employees who like and respect management will try even harder when their leaders are away because they don't want to disappoint their bosses. Conversely, micromanagers and managers who aren't respected (or may even be despised) will often find that employees slack off when management is out of the office. If you find that employees underperform when you're away from the office, you and your managers may have created a negative work environment that results in employees doing the absolute minimum while you're away.

Based on my experience working with organizations of all sizes, I strongly believe these four attributes point to a single issue – ineffective, uninspiring leadership. If even one of these issues is present in your organization, it's time to take a long, hard look in the mirror – and at the managers working under you.

Peak Performance Chapter Activities:

1) Which of the four signs of poor leadership, if any, are present in your organization – or on specific teams within your organization?
2) How can you address these issues to improve the performance of your organization?
3) List all of your employees who left in the past year.
4) Beside their names, list their annual salaries.
5) Now, add up the total of these salaries and multiply this number by .5. This is the amount your organization lost last year because of turnover.
6) How much of an impact would this have made on your organization's bottom line if this number had been added to your revenues or subtracted from your expenses?
7) What can you do to improve the turnover rate in your organization?

Chapter 26: Learning from Mistakes

What I've learned during my career is that life is way too short. There's no reason for me or others to waste our time and efforts with people who simply don't want to learn – or people who don't treat others well.

While this book may make it appear that I've never made mistakes along the way, nothing could be further from the truth. I have made a lot of mistakes. These mistakes are some of the best lessons I've learned. If you've managed people or organizations for any length of time, you have made mistakes, too.

I recently read a post on Facebook from my best friend in college, Jim Bissett, who wrote that even when I served as editor of the college newspaper, "The Columns," at Fairmont State back in 1980, I was already a good manager.

Actually, I wasn't.

Like any other young manager, I didn't always see the big picture or do an effective job of delegating work and trusting my staff. I was more like a coach who barks out orders than a facilitator who brings people together. In my early 20s, I was immature and wasn't fully prepared to lead other staff members, although they were college students, too. But as is the case with every management position I've had, I learned from this experience, too.

During my career, I have been angry, stubborn, stressed and frustrated just like any other person. On numerous occasions, I've talked too much and listened too little. I'm a flawed human, just like everyone else, and at times I certainly haven't managed while "in spirit." Yes, I've made a lot of mistakes, professionally and personally.

The truth is that with every position I've held, I have picked up a little more insight about effective management, some of which I have shared in this book. And through it all, I have tried my best *not* to make the same mistake twice.

Each of the people I consider to be the my key mentors – including Nancy Smithson, Jim Earwood, Jim Frazier, Jack Runion, Doug Walters, Jorea Marple, Pamela Scaggs, J.B. Schramm and Brian Gaines – taught me something vitally important that made me a better human being and more effective leader.

I've also worked with and have seen the efforts of a few uninspiring, ineffective managers during my career. They taught me, too – what *not* to do and how *not* to manage.

My career has been one long, meandering path of personal and professional growth. While it feels extremely gratifying to be nearing the end of this part of my life, the journey itself is what has been most enjoyable.

I've lived, I've learned. I have grown so much through it all.

△ △ △

The most difficult job any manager or executive ever does is hiring great people, which is the first and most important part of any process to create a peak-performing organization. While you can ask every question during numerous interviews and use various personality tests to determine an employee's suitability for a particular role, hiring mistakes can and will be made. Yes, I've made numerous mistakes during my career.

Here's one example.

During one phone interview I conducted years ago, the candidate made an off-hand comment that most would consider to be a little inappropriate, especially for a first interview. I thought the comment may have been made because the candidate was a little nervous.

After putting this very ambitious and dynamic person through an extensive in-person interviewing process and not seeing additional red flags, I believed there was no way this candidate would fail.

Unfortunately, he didn't last in the organization more than a year. I wish I had paid more attention to the very clear red flag about his communication skills!

The lesson I learned is that if there are any signs that make you wonder if the person is a fit for the job – any signs whatsoever – never make the offer. Move on to the next candidate.

I know at times you just want to hire someone – anyone – because your organization may have too much work to do and too few people to get it done, but hiring the wrong person is never the answer. Since this mistake (and a few others I made before this one), I have adhered strictly to the "no red flags" rule with every employee I've hired.

△ △ △

Having worked for a number of organizations, I have also learned to keep an eye out for those same red flags when interviewing for a management position.

I vividly remember interviewing for a job with an organization several years ago. At my first interview, members of the executive team leading the interview were late. On the second interview, they were late again. At my third and final interview, they were a few minutes late once more. Seeing key leadership routinely arriving late and not respecting candidates' time should have been a huge red flag.

I saw similar red flags with a very large organization I interviewed with years ago in the education field. After a lengthy interview process, I was offered an executive management position by the organization's second in command when we met at a local restaurant. Once the offer was officially made, I politely asked if I could use the weekend to consider the offer and talk to my family about the opportunity. The conversation up until that point was very positive, and I thought the position would provide me a wonderful opportunity to grow professionally and advance my career.

The offer was made late on a Friday afternoon. I asked this executive if I could let him know my decision first thing Monday morning.

I believe his exact response was, "Well, if you have to think about it, maybe you're *not* the right person for the job!!"

I could actually see blood rushing to his face in anger. He was clearly *offended* that I wasn't *honored* enough to accept the job right then and there.

I couldn't believe that this leader was so arrogant that he wouldn't allow a potential new executive in his organization to have "over the weekend" to make a major career decision.

I replied, "Given your response, and your need to know something today, I think I can give you my answer. I will not be accepting this job. Thank you very much for the offer, though."

This executive was completely dumbfounded that I had turned him down. He angrily stormed out of the restaurant.

Thankfully, I paid attention to that red flag.

While a red flag should encourage you to walk away from a potential candidate you're thinking about hiring, it should also persuade you to walk away from a potential management opportunity. If it doesn't feel right in your gut, whether you're hiring someone or being hired, walk away and never look back. As my wife tells me all of the time, everything happens for a reason.

Through a few mistakes I've made along the way in both hiring people and accepting positions, I've discovered that those instincts and red flags are *never* wrong.

△ △ △

I have also learned that no matter how much I tried to help managers or employees working with me to become successful, they would never thrive if they didn't listen, didn't have the intelligence to learn, or generally just weren't nice people.

MANAGING TO PEAK PERFORMANCE

While the hundreds of employees, managers and executives I have coached, consulted with or managed during my career have listened to my advice and improved their performance, there have been a few along the way who wouldn't listen. My mistake was wasting too much of my time with people who didn't want to learn, when I could have invested significantly more time developing those who truly wanted to grow professionally.

I recall attempting to mentor a fellow manager at one organization. After he was on the job only a couple of weeks and was clearly struggling, I pulled him into a conference room and gave him a few suggestions to focus his attention on efforts that would have the greatest impact on his team's performance. I had been with the organization a couple of years by then and just wanted to help him be successful. He wouldn't listen. He lasted maybe another month before his employment was terminated.

I also tried my best to coach key executives at two different organizations who could never seem to follow my advice. These organizations struggled – and likely will continue to struggle.

One of the most frustrating experiences in my career was coaching a manager who appeared to want to learn and grow, but in reality lacked the core integrity and personality needed to be an effective leader. I later discovered that his asking for mentoring wasn't the result of a sincere desire to improve; he just wanted to be promoted to his next position. He failed miserably in his next position because accumulating power – not becoming a more effective leader – was his only goal.

I've learned that you can't fix a lack of intelligence or common sense and you can't change people who inherently treat others horribly or don't have core integrity. You can coach nearly any skill to anyone willing to learn and put forth the effort, but there are a few intrinsic qualities that can't be altered in those you manage or mentor no matter how hard you might try.

There's no reason for any of us to invest our time and effort with people who simply don't want to learn or people who don't want to treat others well. As much as I might want to help others become more successful, a few will *never* listen.

I have always believed that a positive attitude and a strong work ethic are much more important than tremendous talent. Time and time again in my career, I have seen that teams comprised of people who have a "can do" attitude and are willing to work hard can achieve significantly more than those with prestigious pedigrees who might have a negative outlook on life and work.

Looking back on my career in its entirety, my biggest mistakes (and regrets) are when I could have stood up even more forcefully for what I believed in at the time. If I had a "do over," I would travel back to those couple of occasions and stand up even more *emphatically* for what I knew was the correct course of action.

Yes, I've learned a lot and I've made mistakes along the way. By sharing a little of what I've learned through this book, I hope I can help to prevent you from making the *same* mistakes.

△ △ △

In my consulting business today – after a long career working for others – I now only work with *select* people and organizations that treat their employees and customers/clients very well, want to learn how to become *more* successful and are inherently "good people." By being very particular, I am able to provide quality marketing, business development, community engagement and public relations support to organizations at one-third to one-half the price what my valued clients would pay anyone else with even half the experience.

I *win* by only working with great people, which makes my life so much easier and happier. They *win* by paying significantly less for professional consulting services. This is definitely a win-win!

Is this effective – being very selective? One company's management I do consulting work for informed me that their year-to-date revenues by early July in the first year I worked with them had exceeded their revenues for the *entire previous year*. Another company I am currently doing consulting work for is actually getting *too much work*, if that's even possible in today's world.

I'm working less, but only working with great people and organizations, and making enough money to enjoy my life. I have to admit that it feels absolutely wonderful to be at this point in my life and career – helping quality organizations and people grow.

My work today isn't about how much money I can earn, but how much of a difference I can make working with really good people and their organizations.

That's a great place to be – for anyone!

△ △ △

While in Boy Scouts nearly 50 years ago, I learned a valuable lesson that I have remembered throughout my entire career. On one of our first camping trips, my father, who was Scoutmaster, told the Scouts as we were preparing to break camp and head home that we should "Leave it better than how we found it."

Although there was some trash around the camp before we arrived, we picked all of it up and took it home in trash bags. There wasn't any firewood for us when we got to the camp, but we made certain the next campers would have enough wood to get their first fire started if they arrived after dark. While there were tracks in the dirt and mud of former campers when we arrived, we used pine branches to sweep over their tracks and ours, erasing most of the evidence that humans had even been there.

Yes, we made the place better than how we found it.

I've remembered this lesson at every stop in my journey and even now as a consultant – the importance of making every place better than when I arrived.

I have tried my best to make a difference – even with a few who didn't want to learn – and I've learned something in every position I've held – even when I made a few mistakes along the way.

Peak Performance Chapter Activities:

1) List the employees in your career who have failed to succeed in the organizations you managed.
2) Beside each name, list the reason for their failure, whether it was attitude, intelligence, integrity or laziness.
3) What have you learned as a manager in terms of which employees will or won't be successful?

4) Use what you've learned to improve your hiring process so you won't waste your time with people who won't be successful.
5) Are you leaving your current organization better than the way you found it?
6) How?

Chapter 27: Pulling It All Together

This was the final and most difficult transformation to make as I led my teams, but it was also the most gratifying.

I know I've rambled quite a bit in this book, touching on a wide variety of subjects and sharing a number of personal stories, all of which are designed to help you become a better, more effective manager.

You have now read nearly an entire volume of information that can guide managers and executives in any organization, from large corporations to small businesses, non-profits and even government agencies or school systems. I have discussed nearly every management topic relevant to each and every one of these sectors at some point in this book – from how to grow revenues, to bringing new employees on board, the importance of developing detailed processes, and even how to track and analyze data. I have shared dozens of anecdotes based on personal experiences and what I've seen during my career to show you rather than just tell you.

I hope that "Managing to Peak Performance" has provided you with sage, easy-to-understand, common sense advice. This guidance can help to shape *any* manager or executive, whether leading a non-profit organization of five employees or a for-profit corporation with 5,000. I believe that every manager or executive, no matter where he or she is leading, will be able find numerous golden nuggets of wisdom in this book.

But if I had to boil my entire management philosophy down to three succinct points, what would they be?

Focus on being a great coach

In the second chapter of this book, I discussed how I transformed an elementary basketball team that hadn't won a game the entire regular season into a team that nearly won the post-season tournament.

First, I had to utilize the talents on my team to make the best, most efficient use of team members' strengths, while minimizing their weaknesses.

Secondly, I focused on the fundamentals, making the complex very simple, then emphasized through positive reinforcement how I wanted my players to perform.

Next, I instilled in my team an unwavering belief that we would be successful. This was probably the most difficult step to achieve, but by recognizing and celebrating even incremental progress, my players began to *believe* that they could win.

As I have managed teams throughout my career, I have always remembered these three key components of becoming a more effective coach and manager.

Focus on developing your employees

In the seventh chapter, I discussed how I changed from being concerned about my own career to begin focusing my attention on developing employees. I changed my focus from *me* and *my career* to *them* and *their careers*. I began managing people as though I wanted them to be working with me five or even 10 years in the future. In short, I took a longer-term view of my employees' professional development.

I began searching for opportunities to help my employees grow, even to the point of giving up the spotlight so that others could bask in the glow of our teams' accomplishments. I purposefully readied my employees for their next positions because I viewed them as the essential assets that would allow our organization to sustain and grow, even long after I was gone.

I tried to share what I had learned in my career to prepare employees for other opportunities that would allow them to advance their careers. I felt gratification from seeing my employees thrive, whether it was in their current organization or in a future one.

It wasn't about *me* anymore; it was all about *them*!

Focus on facilitation
In the 15th chapter, I detailed the third transformation in my management style. I started to see myself as more of a "guide on the side" than the "sage on the stage." I began to view my role to be that of a skilled facilitator, who could bring people together and encourage a collaborative decision-making process.

At some point, I actually began enjoying the occasions I surrendered my "power" to others so that they could lead our team meetings and even decision-making processes.

Now, instead of feeling as though I had to lead *every* discussion, I could sit back, enjoy the interactions, and help guide the dialogue a little by asking a few leading questions or by ensuring that all voices were heard. This was the final and most difficult transformation to make as I led my teams, but it was also the most gratifying.

I didn't always have to be in charge!

△ △ △

As I've shown you throughout this book, many managers and executives are never able to develop the coach's mindset that allows them to see the wide array of talents at their disposal – and the importance of making the best, most efficient use of those abilities. Many managers can't ever make the complex simple, while others fail to inspire their teams to have an unwavering belief in their ability to succeed.

Many are also never able to see themselves as a leader with the responsibility of developing employees, which ultimately limits their organization's performance, growth and sustainability – because they are severely restricting their own employees' professional and personal growth.

And very few leaders are able to make the switch from viewing themselves as "the boss" to becoming more of a "team facilitator," a calm, thoughtful leader who brings people together in a collaborative manner to drive the organization forward – and who can even share facilitation and leadership responsibilities with others.

These three, progressive changes can transform any manager into becoming a more effective leader and one that others will want to follow. I was very fortunate to be blessed with numerous mentors over the past three decades-plus who helped me to evolve to this point.

Using this book and its chapter activities as your daily guide, you can begin this transformation immediately – to becoming the type of leader your employees enthusiastically will *want* to follow.

Peak Performance Chapter Activities:

1) In your current role, how much time do you focus on each area: being a coach, developing employees and facilitating decision-making?
2) Which area do you believe you should focus more of your time on to become a more effective manager or executive?
3) What is preventing you from allowing others to take more of a lead in your organization – their level of development or your mindset? (Realize that either reason is within *your* control.)

Chapter 28: Present because They Were Present

The fact is, I could never bring myself to say that someone "worked for me" when I introduced employees. I always said that they "worked with me."

One of the themes that I've touched on in this book, but haven't yet addressed as a separate issue, is the importance of "being present" when you lead people.

Poor leaders demand great performance; great leaders lead by example. Great leaders are always present, leading the way for their organizations.

What do I mean by "being present?" Allow me to once again *show* you rather than *tell* you.

When I worked with North Carolina Power/Virginia Power and directed communications during numerous crises, including major hurricanes, I would work an average of 16 hours a day until all customers had their power restored. I would provide regular updates on our restoration efforts, not because it was my job to be in the office so much, but because I cared enough about our customers to ensure they had the latest, most accurate information.

During my tenure at this utility, I directed communications for probably 75 hurricanes and tropical storms. Seventy and even 80-hour weeks were routine during these crises, as I would distribute press releases for the 7 a.m. news broadcast, the noon news, the 5 p.m. news and even for the 11 p.m. news. In between, I answered media calls from local, regional and even national news media. I have been quoted in most of the nation's major newspapers and have appeared on national television broadcasts that were covering our hurricane restoration efforts.

In addition to this media relations work, I was also charged with directing our division's community relations efforts throughout our 18,000-square-mile service area. This included speaking in front of civic and community groups, leading our division's employee volunteer program, managing the company's contributions program and participating in numerous civic and educational programs. I was literally on call 24 hours a day, 365 days a year. At the time, I had a company pager, which all managers had the number for in order to reach me if we had a crisis, an outage, or they received a call from the news media.

I remember talking on the phone with one newly-hired district manager from Farmville, Virginia, who questioned if my role as Director of Media/Community Relations was one actually needed in our company. A month or so later, he frantically paged me late one evening after an act of vandalism at one of his substations resulted in a widespread power outage. That night, I returned all the media calls and answered all of the reporters' questions for him, including a few from major newspapers and televisions stations, who questioned if the vandalism was actually "terrorism." This was about the time that global terrorism was starting to become widespread, so this district manager was frantic when he paged me for my assistance.

The next day this same manager called me at my office. "Now I see what you do. I couldn't have made it through this without you. You answered my page when I needed you the most and helped me tremendously!" He was able to see first-hand the quality of service I provided our company, as well as its nine district offices and two power stations.

△ △ △

Let me show you yet another example of the importance of being present.

On January 19, 1994, I was sound asleep at my home in Roanoke Rapids, N.C., when the phone rang. It was Jim Frazier, our North Carolina Power/Virginia Power Southern Division Vice President, on the phone.

MANAGING TO PEAK PERFORMANCE

"Randy, get your butt in here. We have an emergency!"

Still half asleep, I looked at the clock. It wasn't even 2 a.m.

When I arrived at the division office several minutes later, I learned what was happening. We wouldn't have enough electrical capacity when customers woke up in the morning, which created the risk of losing our entire power system – a complete blackout. One of our major generating units had been shut down for unexpected repairs, and an extremely cold day was pushing our system to the limit.

Within a few minutes, I typed and disseminated a press release to the wire services and numerous major media outlets in North Carolina and Virginia. The release explained the dire situation and asked customers to turn off all non-essential appliances when they woke up the next morning. I was the first public relations professional in the entire company to begin disseminating vital information to the public, which helped to save our system from the potential of a system-wide blackout lasting a couple of days. I was "live" on nearly every radio and television station and quoted in nearly every newspaper in our two-state service area.

We protected and saved the power system, because our management team had practiced and planned for just such an event. We had prepared a Load Curtailment Plan that our management team rehearsed quarterly in a tabletop drill, including the media relations component. Our management team had also prepared to implement short rotating blackouts throughout our entire service area in Virginia and North Carolina, which helped us to manage the customer load during that very cold day.

I never thought we would actually use this plan, but we were *thoroughly* prepared.

△ △ △

When I directed communications for Kanawha County Schools, I was typically in the office by 6:30 a.m. every day school was in session, not because it was a job requirement, but because I wanted to be available to communicate with the news media if one of our buses was involved in an accident. I wanted to be able to communicate immediately through the news media with those parents who would be wondering – and worried – if their children were safe. I also wanted my employees who came in later to know that I was there, prepared to lead them every single day.

Randy D. Shillingburg

I remember talking with an elementary principal one day, who asked if my role was vital in the school system, especially in a time of budget cuts and staff reductions. A month or so later, she had an emergency at her school on a Saturday afternoon that resulted in calls from reporters at three television stations and two daily newspapers, which I handled quickly and professionally for her.

She called me on Monday to tell me, "Now I understand what you do."

Later, I wrote a press release about an innovative program at her school, which resulted in widespread, positive media coverage. I also invited key members of her staff on my weekly television news show for Kanawha County Schools to discuss their inventive program, which generated additional recognition. After witnessing the positive impact for her school and on the morale of her staff, the principal thanked me profusely and reiterated how she now saw my role as vitally important for such a large school system.

I was present in all of those schools. In fact I visited every one of nearly 100 schools in my first year on the job with Kanawha County Schools.

While serving as shift manager for the major customer service center, I worked long hours, too, but, more importantly, I walked the floor to interact with my managers and employees. They knew I was present, because they saw me every single day and I interacted daily with my employees and managers. I could tell just by the "buzz" on the floor how well my team was performing. All of the employees knew me by my first name.

I was typically the first employee in our College Summit West Virginia office, when I served as Executive Director. Selling our services and products to schools, I would travel from one end of the state to the other, often in the same week. My team and I didn't leave a single stone unturned in terms of selling to school districts, providing exemplary service to schools or meeting with potential philanthropic partners. We were not going to fail!

When I began managing teams all over America for College Summit, I would board a plane at 5:30 on a Monday morning and return Thursday evening or Friday, not because I enjoyed traveling so much, but because I knew it was important for teams across the country to know that I appreciated them, recognized their hard work and strongly supported their efforts.

MANAGING TO PEAK PERFORMANCE

I have to admit that on a few Monday mornings I would wake up from a nap on the plane, not knowing for several seconds where I was heading that particular week.

I would literally try to remember where I had been the two previous weeks in order to determine where I was in the rotation of visiting and working with all of my teams. I remember one week in particular, when I attended an evening function supporting our Los Angeles team at the University of Southern California, before catching a red-eye flight out of LAX in order to be at another event by mid-morning, this one to support our very talented Indianapolis team.

Those same teams knew that they could call or email me nearly anytime if they needed assistance, and I would help. Whether I was preparing to board a plane early in the morning or working out at the Charleston YMCA on a weekend, they knew they could call or email me and I would respond immediately –or as soon as I was available.

While serving as Director of Operations for a public relations firm, I implemented an emergency notification system in the event any of our clients ever needed our assistance on a night or weekend. The company's phone would be answered by a service that would then call our staff. I was the first person on the list for the answering service to call, because I wanted to be present – and also because of my extensive background in crisis communications for a wide variety of organizations.

△ △ △

While working with The Education Alliance, a West Virginia non-profit, my role was to manage the organization's Partnerships in Education program, which entailed strengthening school-business partnerships across the state. After accepting this position, I established a personal goal of not just doing the absolute minimum, but to actually *transform* partnerships across an *entire* state. To accomplish this, I vowed to work with partnerships in every one of the 55 counties in West Virginia. It took me over a year to accomplish this goal, but I worked in every county school system, helping to improve the quality of collaboration among school and business representatives all over the state.

My extensive travel and work was recognized by the FBI, which recognized me with the FBI Director's Award for Community Service. Even to this day, if I see school or business leaders I worked with in this role, they will tell me that the

Partnerships in Education program was at its pinnacle when I had the privilege of working with so many committed school and business representatives all over West Virginia.

Representatives from our school and business partners across the state did this great work. I only provided the impetus and leadership to help *them* transform *their* partnerships. I was nothing more than a coach, just as I have strived to be throughout my entire career.

The award I received from the FBI was in reality *their* award because of *their* hard work.

I have been truly blessed to work with so many dynamic, enthusiastic, caring people during my career – people who worked extremely hard *with* me. They provided me with the honor of serving *them* during my career. My philosophy has always been that if I expected the best from my employees and the people I served in all of my roles, I always had to give them *my* best.

The truth is that during my career, no one has ever worked *for* me; all have worked *with* me. No one ever served me; it was my pleasure and honor to serve *them*.

My ego would never allow me to say that anyone "worked *for* me" when I introduced employees. I would always say that they "worked *with* me." It may appear to be a minor difference, but it was significant to me. When any manager ever tells me that someone "works for" him or her, I wonder if these words are chosen because of a huge ego.

Whatever I have achieved in my career is because I've had the privilege of working with and at times leading great people. They made *me* look good, they inspired *me*, and they challenged *me* to be my best.

While it may appear that I was never able to enjoy a work-life balance, I actually did – and doing so made me a much better manager. I taught both of my sons how to read before they entered kindergarten, was involved in their school activities, coached their soccer teams, taught my sons how to sail, and took them with me often when I traveled.

The fondest memories I have as a parent are those many weekends on our sailboat, with my two young boys bringing a friend or two for the weekend.

I still remember my *strict rules* about jumping off the boat that I established for our sailboat. I told my sons, who always wore lifejackets when the boat was moving, that they could only jump off the boat into the water on two occasions: 1) If they became so overheated that they couldn't stand the summer heat any longer, or 2) If they just felt like it.

Yes, they *always* adhered to my stringent rules!

What I've discovered is that even those people with the busiest schedules will find time to be involved in family activities, while those who don't want to be active parents and spouses will somehow find excuses, even if their calendars aren't full. I have hopped on a plane at 5 a.m. and flown from one coast to the other so I wouldn't miss one of my son's activities.

Sadly, I've seen a few parents who were unwilling to drive even five minutes out of their way on their way home to attend one of their children's sporting events or band concerts.

△ △ △

I look back now on my life and career with a sense of accomplishment and also a great fondness for those I've worked with along the way. With only a couple of exceptions among the *thousands* of people I have worked with, I would choose to work with the same people all over again – if somehow I were given the chance.

I could easily name a few hundred people whom I have had the honor of interacting with during my life and career.

These wonderful co-workers, clients, supporters, mentors and great friends include: Paul Cartwright, Jim Cartwright, Junior McGinnis, Robert Pyles, Dave

Randy D. Shillingburg

Sanders, Mary Ellen Haney, Margaret Holloway, Cindy Odom, Janet Runion, Kathy Woofter, Stan Donald, Jim Earwood, Billy Joe Wooten, Jim Frazier, Jack Runion, Wade Nelms, Scott Schwebke, Walt Petruska, Rob Jett, Paul Shemansky, Fernando Ibanez, Tom Harp, George Beckett, Doug Walters, Jorea Marple, Donna Talbert, Greg Cork, Steve Scheier, Kristin Abbe, Emily Newman, Alexandra Quinn, Nicole Whiting, Sara Bassell, Lori Cole-Boyce, Jennifer Goddard, Pam Scaggs, Salli Gaddini, Brian Gaines, Blair Taylor, Forrest Wilder, Jayme Waldeck, Jody Pauley, John Happs, Lori Naydock, Susan Bross, Pat Hunter, Harold Miller, Eric Ryan, John Parker, Garth Faile, Craig Grooms, J.T. Ferguson, Aaron Wade, Keri Ferro, Derek Barnett, Dwight Huell, Alexis Shah, Dave Seman, Wendy Vandersluis, Ferdinand Gojani, Rishi Jaitly, Sheree Downey, Dan Foster, Jim Bissett, Linda Elmer, Rhonda Sturm, Rose Heston, Josie Plachta, Jim McCloskey, Clyde Wells, Lynette Maselli, Scott Saxton, Charles Roskovensky, Rose Roskovensky, Brad Rowe, Ed Maier, Shannon Edwards, Kelly Merritt, Bob Berryman, Adam Rosas, YaKima Rhinehart, Becky Goodwin, Margaret Teahan, Creed Holden, Lewis Small, Amber Ullman, Suzie White, Jack McClanahan, Dorothy Moore, Sheldon Maye, Bill Clark, Loretta Wiatr, Brad Giddens, Robi Lombardo, Allen Staggers, Lisa Yoffee, Julie Cipriani, Judy Madden, Christie Mitchell, Shaterri Casteel, Donna Fleming, Karen Larry, Blue Telusma, Melissa Federico, Scott Kaminski, Sonia Mucarsel, Jane Dumire, John Veasey, Brian Summers, Gary Linnen, Tom Bloss, Jennifer Giaquinto, Loubert Senatus, Jeraul Mackey, Nancy Doak, Gail Miller, Marysue Knowles, Susan Shew, Billy Burdette, Hazo Carter, Donna Casto, Paul Collins, Darin Kenley, Nancy Lenhart, Les Atkins, Orlando Espinosa, Georgia Gillette, Jay Gregory, Harold Chandler, Sara Spanier, Laquita Harris, Lloyd Jackson, John Capriotti, Russ Lorince, Chuck Critchfield, Nancy Smithson, Buck Smithson, Julie Mork, John Mork, Kyle Mork, Sean Murray, Ezra Shay, Mertie Shay, Jim Dewar, Phyllis Dewar, Newton Thomas, Rachel Ramos, Jeremiah Ashbaugh, Charles Wilson, T.J. Ravis, Sarah Elliott, Robyn Scates, Judy Pratt, Ivan Barron, Mora Segal, Pam Myers, Rob Spackey, Michael Gemm, Jessica Gemm, Vonda Matthews, Jennifer Albinson, Becky Swiger, Aaron Wade, Blair Dotten-Haley, Bill Walton, Ben Shew, Tony Smedley, Earl Telliga, Dave Stewart, Joel Bailey, Eva Teig Hardy, Michele Koury, Russell Bolyard, Brian Osborn, Joe Myers, Kent Pauley, Chris Ilardi, Rich Tafel, Kevin O'Dell, Rick Usery, Zenobia Edwards, Perry Green, Beth Freeman, Lisa Circle, Amber Bailey, Danny Adams, Renee Dillon, Josh Hinerman, Donna Boyd, Loran Davis, John Cochran, J.B. Schramm, Derek Canty, Steve Paine, Millie Fornell, Sandra Chapman, Lloyd Andrews, Michael Magnaye, Kaici Lore, Monica Bintz, Jim MacCallum, Priscilla Haden, Omar Garriott, Tamika Gordon, Genaro Esposito-Montanez, Cleo Mathews, Jo O'Connell, Dan Dobin, Oudete Taylor, Stacy Lewis, Beth Rehbock, Bridget Bradburn, Nikki Kinder, Tyler O'Dell, Keith Woods, Colin Reger, Kristin Staubly, Dave Stackpole, Tony Slabaugh, Stoney Chaffin, Steve Jones, Karl Brack, Stacy Clay, David Melendez, Onuka Ibe, Rick Johnson, Chris Lawrence, Dale

MANAGING TO PEAK PERFORMANCE

McMillion, Steve Bishop, Jenny Murray, Vanessa Lillie, Kevin O'Shaughnessey, Jose Silva, Zenia Henderson, Rusty Crites, Anne Crites, Diana Long, Chris Smith, Steve Fischer, Holly Henry, Bill Estok, Vana Sendling, Michelle Tafel, Karen Taylor, Erica Allman, Kennie Bass, Dale Witte, Danny Noel, Jonathan Carmenate, Kim Link, Troy Body, Veronica DeLandro, Sunya Young, David Howard, Dean Furbush and Keith Frome – just to name a few who *immediately* come to mind.

I would never be able to forgive myself if I didn't also mention the caring, dedicated teachers and staff at Tunnelton High School, who provided their students in this K-12 school with a world-class education. They gave me and thousands of others a *great* start and a strong foundation of *quality* education. The educators and staff who *immediately* come to my thoughts include: Gerald Cline, Rachel Zinn, Bob Williams, Randy Zinn, Wilma Estep, Lucille Baylor, Ed Fortney, Ira Frame, Robert Cornwell, Wayne Miller, Jean Fortney, Janice Pierce, Sherley Wolfe, Ed Baylor and my sister, Anita Shillingburg.

A few of the people I have recognized above are no longer with us on this Earth, but that doesn't mean I could overlook their contributions to my life and career – or what they still mean to me today.

I was *present* because all of these people (and many more) were *present*, inspiring me every step of the way with *their* great work. As I look over these names once more, I realize just how truly blessed I have been to work with and to be shaped by all of these wonderful people – and hundreds more.

While my career isn't over just yet, I can see the light at the end of the tunnel – And it's approaching fast. I am very proud to have been able to make this incredible journey with – but mostly because of – so many truly amazing people.

While I know I can't personally thank everyone for their contributions to my life and career, I wanted to recognize as many people as I could through these printed pages.

Thank you!

Peak Performance Chapter Activities:

1) List five ways that you show your employees every week that you are more "present."

2) List five more ways you can demonstrate to your employees in the next month that you are more present in helping them and your organization be successful.
3) Among those you work with every day, who do you respect and appreciate the most?
4) How can you show them more often that you respect and appreciate them?

Epilogue: They Won't Have a Chance

This team exemplifies the how and why of my entire career, as well as why I have always been able to lead winning organizations.

In the early 1990s, North Carolina Power/Virginia Power was one of several electric utilities sponsoring an electric car competition in the mid-Atlantic region of the U.S. The winner of the regional competition would travel to Phoenix for the right to be named the national winner. At the time, I was working as Director of Media and Community Relations for the company in its Southern Division headquarters in Roanoke Rapids, North Carolina.

At first, the higher-ups at the corporate headquarters didn't want to sponsor a team in North Carolina. They had selected only highly-respected and award-winning career and technical schools in Virginia to represent our company.

But after months of begging and prodding by our local management team, the senior vice presidents in Richmond *finally* relented. We were reluctantly allowed to select a team, but no one in the corporate offices expected our team to be able to compete against teams with significantly more resources and much more talent – on paper. I remember being told by a least one senior manager at our Richmond, Virginia, headquarters: "They won't have a chance."

After finally receiving this very reluctant approval from headquarters to have a team in North Carolina, I contacted my closest friend in education, John Parker, who worked in the central office of Northampton County Schools, a very rural school system in northeastern North Carolina. He immediately thought of two people to lead the effort at Northampton County High School-East: Eric Ryan, a young, energetic Teach for America participant; and Harold Miller, who I would affectionately describe as a lovable "old school shop teacher" that had apparently been talking about building an electric car for many years.

How rural was Northampton County-High School-East? It was surrounded by corn fields on all sides. It also happened to be in one of the poorest counties in all of North Carolina.

While the students from the larger career and technical centers in Virginia and neighboring states may have had significantly more resources, the teachers and students at that small Northampton County high school had something much more important – grit. They worked numerous nights and weekends, begged and borrowed to obtain the best parts for their electric car, and held community fundraisers just to give themselves a fighting chance. The Ford Escort they built and powered with batteries was appropriately called, "Shocker."

When the North Carolina team arrived at Richmond International Raceway for the competition, they were immediately overwhelmed by the professional paint jobs, numerous corporate sponsorship stickers and fancy trailers assembled by their counterparts in Virginia and surrounding states. The other teams were more like "NASCAR," while our team looked like "dirt track."

One competitor condescendingly asked the Northampton County shop teacher if Shocker were held together by bailing wire. The "city slickers" with all of the money and the colorful, NASCAR-like paint jobs on their cars clearly didn't think this team from rural North Carolina had any chance whatsoever.

But what this team lacked in resources, it made up for in preparation and hard work. Students driving the car were trained by local race car drivers how to drive their car most efficiently on the back roads of Northampton County. The team put a lot more sweat and dollars into what was "under the hood" than the slick paint, corporate sponsorships and fancy trailers.

In each event held over a three-day period, the Shocker team consistently placed first or among the leaders and was named the overall winner at the end of the competition. This team from the most rural high school in the entire competition outperformed the larger, more prestigious and better-funded schools to won the regional competition!

If this were the end of the story, it would be an inspiring one. But this same team traveled to Phoenix and surprised teams from all across America, winning the *national competition*. This story was so incredible, so inspiring, that it is now told in a nationally-distributed book, "Electric Dreams," written by Caroline Kettlewell. Not only did this competition change the lives of the students and teachers involved, but it also helped to transform this poor, rural county. One of the students on this team, a young lady, was the first African-American female to ever race on a NASCAR track.

This project changed lives in Northampton County and throughout the entire region!

The last time I communicated with Eric Ryan, he informed me that Disney had contacted him about making this feel-good story into a nationally-distributed movie!

To be completely honest, I did very little to help this team – except for advocating strongly with corporate leaders to give them a chance to compete, picking an educator/friend who selected the right people to lead it, and letting team members know every step of the way that I believed in them.

I look back and consider this electric car team to be one of the highlights of my career. Students from even the poorest, most rural areas of America can compete and win – if only given a chance and a little belief.

△ △ △

This talented, nearly-overlooked team exemplifies the *how* and *why* of my entire career, as well as *why* I have always been able to lead winning organizations. I didn't do the work, but I provided others with the opportunity to be successful. I've always believed in underdogs, perhaps because I was one.

As the Miracle Mets' Tug McGraw said many years ago, "Ya gotta believe."

Throughout my career, I *have* believed that the teams I worked with or led could achieve anything – if only given half a chance to compete.

No one likely believed my elementary basketball team had even a remote chance of making it to the championship game in the postseason tournament, after not winning even a single game in the regular season.

No one probably believed that an electric utility could turn around its horrific public perception, after being asked to leave the state by the Governor of North Carolina.

Very few people probably thought one "newbie" manager with inexperienced managers working under him would outperform managers with significantly more experience in a production environment.

No one likely believed that we could transform the Communications Department for West Virginia's largest school system into a true public relations and communications division.

No one probably believed that some guy who grew up in Preston County could be doing public relations consulting work for several of the largest corporations in America – or training plant managers from all over the world.

No one likely believed that an unheralded team from one of the poorest, most rural states would be the first to prove a sophisticated business model developed by a few of the greatest minds in the social change arena.

Only a few visionaries probably thought that College Summit teams could transform the college-going culture for low-income students all over America.

And I would say that no one else believed that a group of kids from one of the poorest, most rural school districts in America could ever build an electric car, yet alone win regional and national competitions against dozens of the most prestigious and well-funded vocational and technical schools in the entire country.

I believed.

I have *always* believed.

I have always had unwavering faith that the impossible is possible. I have always believed in the almost mystical power of a team of thoughtful, hard-working, committed people working together to achieve greatness. While I knew that I could accomplish very little by myself, I have always believed that the teams I worked with or led could achieve *anything*!

I hope that I have been able to show you that the impossible is possible – and that managing yourself and others to peak performance should be your goal each and every single day.

www.ingramcontent.com/pod-product-compliance
Lightning Source LLC
Chambersburg PA
CBHW032007170526
45157CB00002B/587